PEDRO'S PROGRESS

Pedro's Progress
A SECULAR PILGRIMAGE

Nicholas Ricketts

ISBN: 9798335061872

Copyright © 2024 Nicholas Ricketts

All rights reserved. No part of this publication may be reproduced, distributed, or transmitted in any form or by any means, or stored in a database or retrieval system, without the prior written permission of the copyright holder, except by a reviewer who may quote brief passages in a review.

For G.

CONTENTS

Prologue 11

1 THE MULE	14	
2 ON THE START LINE	18	
3 HEADING DOWN	24	
4 TURNING LEFT	29	
5 THAT RIVIERA TOUCH	35	
6 NIGHT BOAT TO PATRAS	41	
7 LOUTAKIA	48	
8 TO PIRAEUS	54	
9 NEA MONI	60	
10 CHIOS TOWN	66	
11 SIREN CALL	74	
12 A LITTLE BIT OF TOAST	81	
13 INTO GREAT BEAUTY	88	
14 THE CALL OF THE OWL	93	
15 HAMMAM AND HAIRCUT	102	
16 TOUR OF DUTY	109	
17 TURKEY LEFTOVERS	114	
18 ISLAND LIFE	122	
19 KASSANDRA CROSSING	138	
20 THESSALONIKI	141	
21 RIDING PELION	148	
22 PLAIN TALES OF THE HILLS	155	
23 VOLOS CITY	159	
24 LIP SERVICE	163	
25 NORTH BY NORTHWEST	168	
26 PIZZO MY HEART	173	
27 SWEET SICILIA	179	
28 EUREKA	185	
29 IN DOCK	190	
30 DAYTRIPPER	197	
31 PER SARDINIA	201	
32 CAGLIARI KICK BACK	206	
33 THE HILL	211	
34 ISLAND CROSSING	218	
35 THE TRUMAN SHOW	223	
36 AN IDEA OF ITALY	230	
37 CORSE TREATMENT	234	
38 BASTIA RETREAT	238	
39 FRENCH CONNECTION	242	
40 HOT STUFF	249	
41 BACK IN THE 8TH	256	
42 ALL SAINTS	260	
43 A MUSÉE	263	
44 LENS OF HISTORY	268	
45 ADIEU	273	

Epilogue 278
Acknowledgements 280

England
HOME
MARLOW
FOLKESTONE
ARRAS
PARIS
France
DIJON
BOURG -EN- BRESSE
MONT BLANC TUNNEL
Italy
MODENA
NICE
BASTIA
BONIFACIO
ALGHERO
CAGLIARI

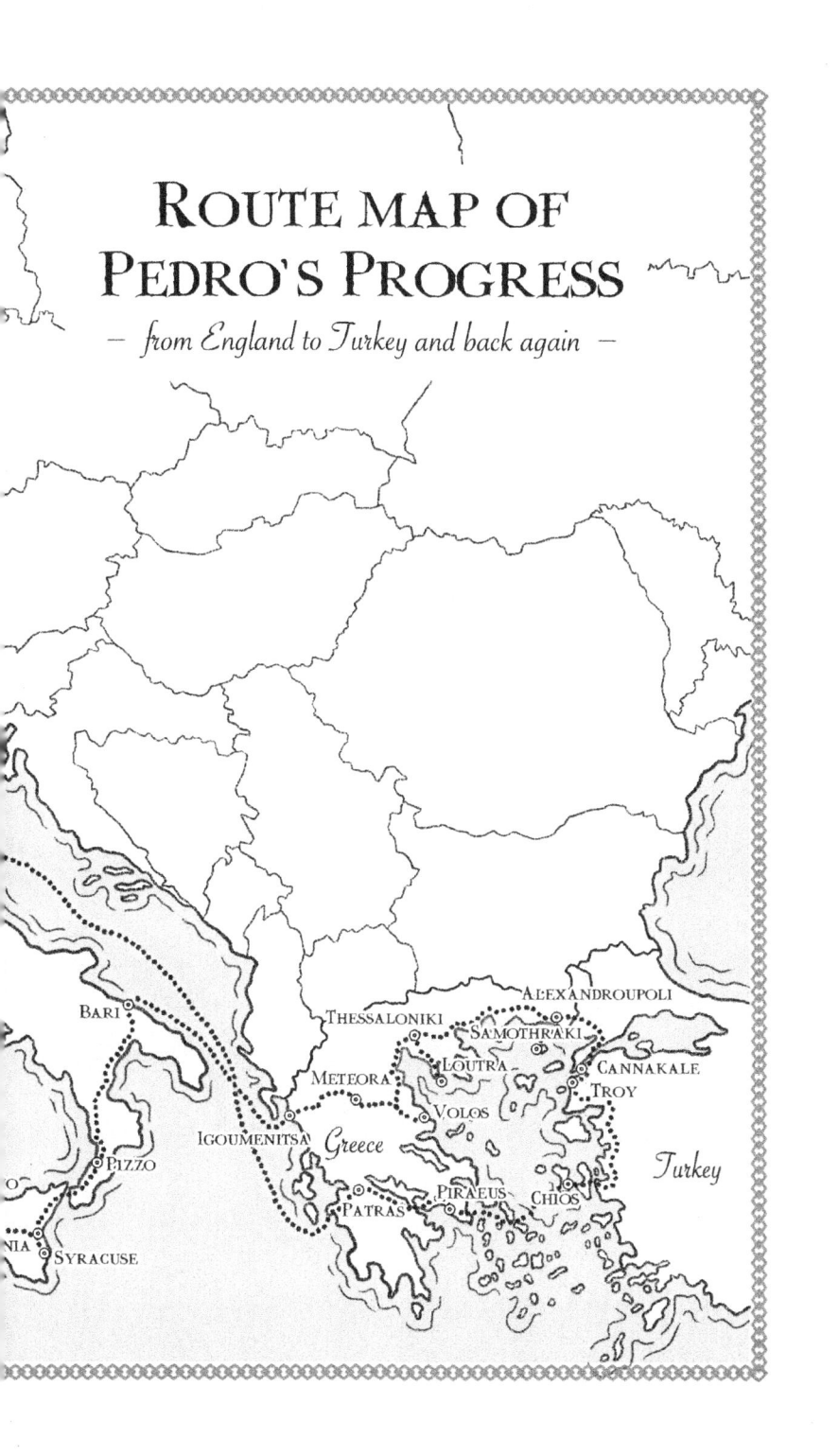

Route Map of Pedro's Progress
– from England to Turkey and back again –

ALEXANDROUPOLI
BARI
THESSALONIKI
SAMOTHRAKI
METEORA
LOUTRA
CANNAKALE
TROY
VOLOS
IGOUMENITSA
Greece
Turkey
PIZZO
PATRAS
PIRAEUS
CHIOS
SYRACUSE

PROLOGUE

In the late afternoon we crested a rise and there it was laid out before us. A strong feeling of déjà vu. But where from? A dream? I let out the clutch and we jounced over the unmade track. Stuff in the back knocking, shocks hissing. We took it easy, avoiding the worst of it. Sometimes with one leg up on the side to prevent grounding. Now and then a thorny and leafless bush scratched down the door with a squeal. How did they survive without leaves? Enough sun to make even a thorn produce nourishment I guessed.

LOOKING TOWARDS LESBOS FROM MAINLAND TURKEY

I stopped mid-track and got out to take it all in, leaving Pedro ticking over, revs rising and falling as if wheezily breathing. I reached in and switched him off, leaving only the white noise of the cicadas.

This was the turning point. We had made our eastings. From now on the sun would be to our port side.

What a view. So beautiful. I knew this is what I had come for. That I had reached a destination of sorts. The land, where it met the sea, was ragged and white and rocky. No beaches. A short way off, a hulking, humpbacked island that looked a bit like a turtle made out of pumice. Whitish grey and dotted with black scrub. No, not scrub, olive trees, that gave it some sense of scale. All around, the sea a creamy blue, turning darker where it met the horizon, covered in white nail trimmings of wavelets. And always the perfect, spotless and graded azure of the sky.

Where had I seen all this before? It matched no memory. Even though the feeling was intense. All those dreams I'd had of looking out to sea, like a lonely wizard on the foreshore, those were of Greece, or so I had thought.

Perhaps this was second time around stuff? Perhaps I had been here before, but in another life? There was something deeply romantic about it. Not just the ancient history that it had seen, but the fact that it hadn't changed in all those millennia. Despite its barren-seeming surface, people had made a life here then and still eked one out today.

The sun on my back was hot, the shadows still short. But there was a gentle breeze now cooling through my baggy, untucked shirt. Searching the edges of the water I looked for signs of where I was headed. I could see the top of something spiky and white. A radio mast perhaps. Then to the left, some shacks in a semi-circle, their roofs covered in dust, making them near invisibly camouflaged against the ground. That must be it, the motel.

I didn't really want to leave this view, so I stayed a little longer. After a while the sun lowered. To lose the light on a road like this would make things tricky. So, I got back in, let off the handbrake and edged the car down the hill in neutral.

1
THE MULE

I had made all sorts of preparations for this trip, but in the end, I did nothing to Pedro. I mean what could go wrong really? Well, anything and everything in fact, with an old car like he was. 14 years old and probably not worth more than a couple of hundred quid, if that. You could spend a small fortune replacing stuff, in a preventative manner, and never know what might go wrong next.

There was the original exhaust – for instance – that had been mentioned as an advisory on every MOT for the past eight years. The tailpipe looked like a stubbed-out cigar, but still it seemed to be hanging in there. Now and again a series of well-timed road undulations would set the rear box banging on its perished rubbers, sounding like Senor Wences' skull in a box trying to get out.

Then there was the radiator. Six years ago, I had poured Radweld into it, a temporary fix to stop a leak. We weren't losing water, and it was still doing okay now.

And there was the rattle from the steering column that – apart from being a little unnerving for passengers – had not really affected the handling.

These were just some of the known issues. I had no clue as to what else could be wrong with the car. But then I told myself that I was only driving Pedro to Turkey. Much of it through western Europe. Where a car like him would be ten a penny and hopefully just as cheap to fix. Certainly nothing serious was going to give out. Tyres good. Brakes working. Oil looked cleanish. So then, time to have faith.

But still I had this nagging anxiety at the back of my mind. I put this down to good engineering sensibility, rather than a premonition of catastrophic failure. I had a word with Pete, my mechanic.

'Where are you off to?' he said.

'Athens and beyond.'

'No problem, he won't let you down.'

The first day would prove that point. I had never driven the car more than 70 miles in any direction, but I'd made my first stop after the channel tunnel Bourg-en-Bresse. Nearly 600 miles from home. A bit of a mission perhaps?

◂•▸

PEDRO, JUST ANOTHER TEENAGER ON THE BEACH

We'd bought – or rather G bought – the car on an autumn day in Aylesbury back in 2009. For around six years we'd managed with just one car, but now she was starting back at work.

A friend of ours had tipped us off that Perry's were 'pushing out Fiat Pandas for five grand dead'. These were what are known in the trade as 'quota cars', priced to go before the end of the month to make the dealership's numbers. We chose the Tiziano Red from the three colours on offer, the others being Vanilla Yellow and Guacamole Green. I had quite liked the guac colour for its quirkiness, but this was vetoed. Years later, when the red paint started peeling off like Michael Gambon's skin in The Singing Detective, I reminded G that it was better to have a car painted the colour of a Mexican dip than a car with no paint at all.

The salesman had sat us down and asked whether we wanted any extras. G and I – who were broke at the time – had already signed a pact in blood on the way over. We'd buy the car for 5k and not a penny more. So naturally I asked if there were any options he'd recommend.

'Well sir, air conditioning is only another hundred pounds.'

'Profligate!' spurted G.

The salesman and I gaped at each other. But she was not to be swayed. The year following the car's purchase proved to be one of the hottest on record. Discretion forbids me saying more.

'Anything else?' I asked just to wind her up a bit more.

'Well, we've never sold one of these without roof rails. They're only twenty-five pounds and I'd like to say that the car looks positively naked without them.'

'Ridiculous!' muttered G. 'What would I want with a roof rack?'

However, by the end of the year, G had also come to the conclusion that the car looked 'positively naked' without roof rails. And so, I fitted them in my slippers and dressing gown as a surprise on a frosty Christmas Day morning. Instead of £25 they cost me £198. But we don't mention that around the breakfast table.

Now, with a wistful sigh, the salesman opened his hire-purchase presentation binder, hoping to at least make a minor profit through an agreement.

'Who is to be the owner of the vehicle?' he asked.

'I will be,' said G.

'And how would madam like to finance the vehicle?'

'Shove it on that,' she said, flipping her credit card across the desk. I appreciated his aplomb, as he keyed the price into the card reader and handed it to her to enter the PIN.

I drove the car home with the windows down and the kids screaming in the back as we squealed the tyres on the hot tarmac. This little donkey handles quite well, I thought, as G angrily flashed her lights at me following closely in our Toyota estate.

'I think we'll call him Pedro, guys.'

2

ON THE START LINE

To be the hero in your own story you need to go on a quest. To make a journey, whether real or imagined. In mythology this is usually about – firstly - crossing a threshold, often guarded by monsters, which the hero must overcome to start out. In your own mind these monsters can take on real tangibility with almost palpable reasons as to why you shouldn't go at all. If you are at all introspective you can convince yourself that to stay put is not just the rational thing to do, but actually a philosophical and reasoned approach. To perhaps sit like a Buddhist monk, reaching enlightenment and Anatta, the complete denial of self. Or like a Proustian character, propped up in bed eating madeleines.

On the other hand, you may be of the opinion that your life is only defined through your interactions with others. In which case, to go out and meet people, and not just acquaintances on the street but other cultures, with languages foreign and various. Where you cannot simply rely on your humour to a passer-by. Where you need to make an effort beyond smiling like a psycho.

If so, then you're up for a challenge. There is no wrong or right way. It is pointless to feel guilty, either about going, or not going.

◆•▶

ONE FOR THE ALBUM

Three in the morning, a Monday. I stood in the hallway looking at myself in the mirror by the dim light of pre-dawn.

It was chilly, mid-September. The rain, which had been continuous since the day Thames Water had announced the hosepipe ban three weeks before, had stopped, temporarily. Behind my head the thermostat

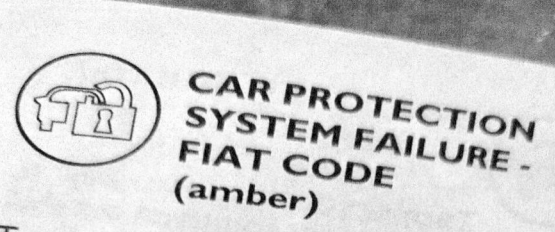

THE FIRST, MEANINGLESS WARNING LIGHT OF THE TRIP

clicked and from the kitchen I heard the dull whump of the boiler defying the cost-of-living crisis and my bank balance. I turned the thermostat down to zero. Looking out at the garden, the hollyhocks - with their blooms the colours of Edwardian knickers - were long gone. At least the grass – on a lawn parched all summer – was growing back. A single sign of hope against all the challenges the country was facing. Britain's beloved Queen had died just three days prior, sending the population into an even more unsettled state. I hooked one strap of the bag onto my shoulder and quietly pulled the door closed. As I walked through the gate, G whistled from the front bedroom window and I blew her a smiling, farewell kiss.

I walked round the corner where Pedro was hunkered down at the kerb. I started him up, and immediately a warning light that I'd never seen before flashed amber. It looked like a padlock, so I assumed one of the doors was open. I opened all five and slammed them. If the neighbours weren't yet awake, they were now. Back in the car the warning light was still on. 'Bollocks!' What could it be? Total hydraulic failure? Perhaps all the oil had drained out overnight? Maybe all four tyres were flat? Hmmm, not sure.' I turned off the ignition and restarted. The light was gone. 'Good!' We drove down the deserted high street and onto the suspension bridge over the river.

Round the M25 it started to get foggy, creating a strange effect. The lighting through the mist caused a curtain of whiteness to form at the edges of the road… but above it was total blackness. A bit like being in a tunnel with illuminated walls.

Then flashing warning lights to reduce speed. There were cameras around, so I thought I'd better. I couldn't see any reason for it and the speed limit was now down to 20 mph, ridiculous on an empty ten-lane highway. I felt very vulnerable in my little car waiting for a huge wagon doing eighty to hit me up the rear.

Finally, Folkestone. The young woman in the French booth stamped my passport and handed it back stifling a yawn, which made us both laugh.

I drove onto the train – Le Shuttle – I thought the French didn't allow such expressions of franglais? Coming to a stop behind two black Range Rovers and a brand-new S-Class Merc, also shiny black. The doors to the compartment closed so it was just us and them. Pedro's scabby roof rather letting the side down. I wondered who the owners could be. Perhaps some sort of diplomatic mission with their blacked-out windows? But out got a man in a baseball cap and very baggy joggers with the crotch at ankle level. He had enough chains for Mr T. I goggled at him, and he came over for a chat. Probably wondering who on earth was driving this piece of crap car in 'his' train compartment.

'Where are you off to?' I asked as a polite opener.

After a heartbeat of hesitation, he replied, 'Paris, innit?'

'Lovely at this time of year.' I breezed.

'Yah man, got the missus in the back and a couple of mates too innit. So why not?'

'Why not indeed' I thought, only then letting my mind turn to how they made their money. It certainly wasn't by selling software. But before I could ask this – potentially awkward – question, the train driver announced that because another train had broken down in our tunnel there would be an hour's delay. Terrific! So much for a 3am start! But, in truth, I couldn't be vexed. Our first experience of mechanical failure was thankfully not Pedro's.

3

HEADING DOWN

Out of the tunnel, off the train and into the French countryside. A strong day of sunshine lay ahead. After a while we passed a brown sign saying 1520 Champ de Drap d'Or.

The Field of the Cloth of Gold had really caught my imagination as a child when I read about it in a magazine called Treasure. It was right here. And exactly five centuries ago. On this scrappy bit of hinterland, a day's ride from Calais. I tried to imagine it. The French and English camps I imagined as striped and pointy tents, like something out a Hollywood period film. But I remembered that it was a serious undertaking, building palaces of canvas to entertain and lists for jousting with grandstands. So much luxury and money was thrown at it the country was practically bankrupted. Oh, for a time machine!

Further on, and through a ride cut through the trees, rose the twin towers of the Vimy Ridge monument, where a lot of Canadians had lost their lives in the First War. I hadn't seen it since the eighties. A friend and I had travelled back from the south of

France after he had chased down his girlfriend, an egg-packer from Leeds. It had left a lasting impression on me, shrouded by mist and ethereally beautiful on the day we'd visited. I could have made a quick detour but I wanted to keep going. We had a long way to travel today. Perhaps we would visit on the way back.

That had been a memorable trip with my friend Teddy and his exhausted Cortina Mk4. We were both 19 at the time. Coming off the ferry on the first night into a pea souper so thick that we were forced to park up in a lay-by. We wound down the seats to catch some zeds and were woken in the morning by the car bucking up and down. The movement was due to a couple of Hell's Angel bikers sitting on the bonnet smoking a joint. We were so terrified that we shut our eyes until we heard them roar off on their Harleys. Teddy's girlfriend we finally located at a campsite in Sete and spent a couple of nice sunny days on the beach. My friend slept off a boozy lunch in his trunks and burned himself badly. His skin came off in sheets on the way back. By the time we got home the girlfriend had fallen for her coach driver and eventually married him. A lucky escape I assured the heartbroken Teddy.

But I couldn't think about all that now. The road was calling me southwards. It was like being pulled on a very long piece of elastic, and I felt deeply optimistic for my journey.

We had stopped for fuel, but the first real stop was Bourg-en-Bresse. Blige me, almost 600 miles on the trip-o-meter and we hadn't been over 80 all day, and I mean <u>all</u> day. The time was now five o'clock. I tied

GET YER PILES 'ERE MISSUS

Pedro to a plane tree in the main square and patted him down for a job well done.

Looking around I thought to myself, why had I chosen Bourg-en-Bresse as the first stop? It had simply looked right on the map. A good place from which to head onwards to Mont Blanc and the tunnel. Also, the home of Poulet de Bresse, a dish I have enjoyed. Unfortunately though, B-en-B is a bit of a drab town apart from the very centre, which was where I was staying.

It was a Monday so most of the restaurants were closed. Some of them until Thursday. Staff shortages or just a normal state of affairs? I didn't bother to ask. I wandered the back streets. Pharmacists, vape shops and an establishment going by the name of Piles Shop. Batteries presumably but I didn't get close. Only a couple of bars open and they were overrun with students.

I finally found somewhere for a beer. In the bar there was a speaker set up broadcasting to the patrons the maunderings of a headsetted panel of tired looking hacks. I asked what this was all about, just as the show closed to desultory and ironic applause. The waiter told me it was the local radio station celebrating their 40th anniversary. Wow, what a Monday night!

With a load more driving planned for tomorrow I thought I'd better get my head down and repaired to the hotel, a pleasant place on the main square. The only accommodation I was to pre-book for the entire trip.

In the conservatory dining room attached to the hotel, I had a ho-hum Magret de Canard aux Morilles, the sauce way too yellow and runny. But the Côte de

Brouilly was pleasant enough. And two rather beautiful girls were serving that night. I was almost alone in the salon. The only entertainment came from the maître d, who shouted several times at a clumsy bus boy for knocking paint off the door frames with his oversized tray held at hat height.

4

TURNING LEFT

Up early and out of town. We drove 'toutes directions'. Through miles of urban sprawl, which the French seem to be so good at creating. I recalled Jonathan Meades describing it very well and have experienced it so many times myself. It seems ridiculous to me that French motorways can be more picturesque than their A road counterparts. These routes are lined with out-of-town, low-rise furniture showrooms and DIY stores. It means that local towns of any character are often linked by a commercial conurbation and lose some of their identity. Le Clerc followed by Monsieur Meuble followed by Citroen followed by MonoPrix and repeat to fade. The planners seem to have opted for an American style of shopping experience where the car is king.

Such were my thoughts in trying to reach the escape velocity required to break out of Bourg-en-Bresse's orbit. Amidst all this, and just before the motorway, I sat at some lights and saw a lovely church. It had one of those multi-coloured tiled roofs, like the famous hospital in Beaune. In front was an elegant manor, a beautiful collection of buildings, sitting in a green sward of clipped lawn. A landscape composition worthy of Corot.

I found out later that it was a religious complex, comprising a church – St Nicolas de Tolentin de Brou – with its roof of glazed tiles, and a royal monastery built at the start of the 16th century for Margaret of Austria. Now it was owned by the state and housed a collection of art.

But, no time to stop. The light went green and a truck with a double trailer on my inside turned left, nearly crushing Pedro against the barrier. We stopped until he'd finished his manoeuvre and then followed him onto the peage.

Onwards to the A40. And a very different A40 to the one that runs west from London where the crash barrier is held together with baling twine. This is the road that goes to the Mont Blanc tunnel. A proper bit of infrastructure with carriageways suspended between gorges and one above the other up the mountainside. An exhilarating drive through low cloud and sunshine.

Nearing the tunnel, a Brit in bright red Aston Martin slowed down and gave me a cheery wave. Pedro is getting noticed more as I go further south. And not everyone is laughing, at least!

Great driving in spectacular country with mountains rising each side and snow on the tops. Just one small 'bouchon' at Annamasse caused by the corporation cutting the verges. You know when you're close to Switzerland when they stop the traffic to mow the grass. Tidy people, those Swiss.

No queue to speak of for the tunnel, which always

surprises me by its length. They are repairing it at night, and it is shut most evenings. It's in a poor state inside despite the major refit after the fire. The ceiling blackened and crusty looking. I wondered if they had really cleaned it properly. I didn't like to think what might be up there. 39 people had died in the fire of 1999, but you could hardly turn it into a memorial. Just like the Kings Cross station fire where 31 died. There's a commemorative clock and plaque in the ticket hall and commuters pass by without a glance. When I saw it, I wondered if they should have set it to the time of the conflagration which I'd narrowly missed myself. But I guess a stopped clock in a train station is not a very helpful thing!

Out the other side and no sign of a border. Was I now in Italy as a post-Brexit illegal alien? I guessed I'd find out when it came to leave on the ferry from Ancona. Note to self, get to the port extra early.

Different drivers now that I was in Italy. Most Italian men seem to see the tollbooth as an F1 pitstop. The usual Italian paradox means that they'll be revving their engines when they see me get out and walk around, but taking as much time as they like to sort coins from backseat passengers when it's their turn. Impatience is the norm but it's not aggressive like you find in the UK.

I drove till I got tired and stopped for a beer. This was 4pm. I'd eaten nothing all day except some rationed wine gums, water and a dodgy coffee in a service station. I'd been cracking the whip. Another 400 miles, and the temperature was rising. We'd driven all day again with the windows down, not very fuel efficient but what was the alternative? The hundred quid we'd saved on the AC seemed more than a fool's economy now. I thought it was enough driving for today and looking at the map, Modena seemed a likely place to make camp.

Modena, spiritual home of Ferrari and Il Commendatore's birthplace. There's a museum full of all things Ferrari here, choc-a-bloc with engines and F1 cars. I guessed this must be a pilgrimage site for the Tifosi. But pristine racing cars in chrome and glass vitrines weren't really my cup of oolong.

By contrast, Pedro was now getting pretty mucky, with a bug-squashed windscreen attracting annoying vespi every time we stopped. So, how nice to have the car filled up by an attendant and the screen professionally washed. I'd pay a small tip for that service anytime back home.

Into Modena. My first impressions were of a jumping little town with evidently plenty of brass about. Substantial in a medieval way with colonnades (that reminded me of Turin) and big brick churches. But a little schizoid for my taste, uncertain whether it is northern or central Italian in its building style.

It was a warm and very humid evening. I found it all a bit claustrophobic and the dead air, whining with mosquitoes, only added to the atmosphere. It is typical of these old Italian cities that despite large public spaces there is nowhere that you can go to escape for fresh air or get a vista.

We parked up and I found a very cheap room in what happened to be a rather swanky hotel. I was later to see it featured in the film Ferrari. My room was not swanky, however. I went out to do a little light exploring.

ONE OF SEVERAL PANELS COMMEMORATING WW2 RESISTANCE
FIGHTERS IN MODENA

In a square I found the impressive romanesque cathedral with its beautiful tower, the Torre della Ghirlandina. An elegant campanile in white stone, nearly 90 metres tall and dating from 1179. I thought about what we were building in Britain at around that time. The square was also where I found a memorial to Modena's partisans who had died resisting the Nazis in WW2. Hundreds of passport-sized photographs in three giant frames made for a poignant display that held my attention far longer than a list would have done.

Time to grab a bite, but for the first time my 'unpassable' Italian was unrecognised. I was a bit annoyed by this. Even I can make myself understood when enquiring after table availability. But there was nothing doing anyway. All the restaurants were full, mostly with Americans. With more Americans queuing. I wondered why? Ah well, no dinner then. Good for the figure!

Wandering the back streets, I settled at a quiet bar and ordered a Campari spritz, which came with small slices of pizza, nuts, crisps and olives. So, dinner after all.

Then two stateside crones arrived at the next table and started talking at the tops of their voices.

'Senta! Por favoray!!'

The waitress approached and asked what they'd like.

The one with the Dame Edna Everage glasses took the hands of the waitress in hers, saying, 'My dear, you just do not know what a day we've had. Four plane journeys. And now we'd like a drink.'

I caught the eye of the waitress whose face was poker professional when the other harridan said. 'You got any of that Spanish wine?'

When she came back later to ask if I wanted a refill, I took the opportunity to enquire if she had any Albanian wine. She wagged a finger at me and returned with another Campari spritz.

It was the end of another long day in the saddle. I got to my room, made a thorough search – with my torch – for mosquitoes, turned the AC up full blast and hit the hay.

5
THAT RIVIERA TOUCH

In the morning there wasn't a lot of room beside the bed to do my 15-minute yoga. But I found by opening both the bathroom door and the wardrobe I could just about fit.

I refilled my water bottles and placed them behind the makeshift bungy cords I'd tied around the passenger seat. Pedro's interior is all hard plastic. The driving experience is a bit like being the pilot in an Airfix model aircraft. Nowhere to put nothing. And anything you did put anywhere – say a pair of sunglasses – would immediately end up on the floor and usually under your clutch foot. Hence the bungy cords, keeping water and emergency wine gums to hand.

Driving styles were getting lax the further I travelled south. The slow lane was evidently considered only for lorries. No Italian driver was to be seen dead in that lane on point of principal. And another strange behaviour which I'd only ever encountered way down south in Italy, driving while straddling two lanes. Was it some half-hearted attempt to use the slow lane or to show intention that you were on that side of the motorway? Not sure. Very erratic driving now with almost all male drivers using their mobile phones. At one point there was a big BMW so close to my rear bumper that I was momentarily unnerved. I moved to the right just as traffic was joining from a junction. I looked to the left but the beemer had immediately closed me out. Three lanes of cars now merged into two to pass under a bridge. Everyone held their breath and somehow, we all slithered onwards without touching.

Further along, on the road outside Ferrara, a terrible smell. Truly awful, like an unflushed toilet, that lingered for almost 20 miles and had me mouth-breathing while wondering if I was imbibing farticles of human excrement. Certainly not anything of animal origin. Perhaps it actually was human. Nightsoil? The rest of the motorway sat in air-conditioned comfort, presumably with their vents on recirc, and oblivious to the stink outside. But it was a very hot day. Shutting the windows was not an option for me.

Around this time, I noticed a slight but high-pitched whine from the front-left wheel. Hmmm, bearing perhaps? Or Pedro keening to be back home? But he was home, wasn't he?

After three hours the road dropped down with lovely views onto the beaches of the Adriatic. I had passed the famous resort of Rimini and was now on the single-lane road into Ancona. Just me and some very large trucks negotiating the twists and turns.

On the right and up the hillside was a lot of earthmoving activity where they were putting in massive foundations for the SS21 Adriatic coast road.

Or so a giant billboard told me. Obviously, it was to be an elevated section of some kind. A tricky undertaking on that steeply banked pasture. But the Italians are noted for their elegant autostrada architecture.

Naturally, with the cost of this new road, they had stopped maintaining the old one. Despite that, it was the port's only arterial connection with the north. It meant some dodging around to skip the potholes. Some of them crater-like and a couple of feet deep. Even the trucks were treating them like roundabouts.

Ancona. Not the prettiest drive in, with stockyards and train freight with overhead power lines blocking views of the sea. But what a great place. I immediately liked it. An honest port town with obvious strategic importance on the Adriatic and the deep integrity of knowing its value. What a contrast to Modena. Open and breezy.

I got parked in a very tight and precipitous underground car park, I couldn't imagine anything bigger than Pedders making it down into the depths. Back in the sunshine I met the charming owner of the Airbnb I had located the night before. It was a brilliantly converted room of an old palazzo on a busy street. Airbnb is always worth the effort, even if it's just for one night. You get to stay in places of such charm, rather than a faceless hotel room.

Quite a large-ish lady, she was wearing a rose-coloured translucent chiffon shift against the heat. Showing me around I asked about air conditioning. She said there was no AC because the building had a conservation order on it, but pointed to an industrial-sized fan which she then demonstrated by turning it on. Unfortunately, this blew her dress up and over her head. I scrabbled to turn it off while she emerged with flushed cheeks. All four of them! My Italian was not up to apologizing for what had been a schoolgirl error on her part. But we had a good laugh about it together.

<•>

THE ADRIATIC PORT OF ANCONA

So then, Ancona. The first thing that strikes you is the size of the churches. They are monumental and rise up the steep hill out of the port.

Obviously, this hints to great wealth at one stage. Before they existed, Roman emperor Trajan had made it his main port with trade from the east and there is still a monumental arch to him standing amidst all the cranes and paraphernalia of the docks.

Ancona is one of the largest natural harbours in Italy and is in the shape of an elbow, hence the name from the ancient Greek, arkon or elbow. Independent – until it merged with the Papal States – it had successfully fought off attacks and sieges from the Venetians, Turks and Austrians.

Stamira, a local heroine who escaped through a gate one night to set fire to the besieging Venetian camp, is commemorated with a statue in the main square.

◆•▶

That night, and in that same piazza, half the town had turned out to listen to a local politician, Sr. Paragone, make a speech. I picked up one of his leaflets which read 'Io Non Dimentico' or 'I'm not barmy'. Personally, I couldn't really tell if he was or not, but he was certainly impassioned, and the crowd were loving his energy.

This was a time of a snap election. When isn't it in Italy? There were concerns in the liberal press that voters would now follow the fallen Draghi government – which had brought financial stability – with a hard-right regime. Gianluigi Paragone had a successful career in TV and radio and in 2020 launched the independent party Italexit with the main aim of getting Italy out of the EU. But, as it turned out, a centre-right coalition led by Georgia Meloni and her radical right Brothers of Italy party won the day, sharing power with Salvini's lot.

◆•▶

As I mooched about, it became apparent that Ancona was quite the civilised town with lovely shops and some stylish restaurants. A very liveable place I thought. I could easily spend a week or two here.

I was a bit guilty that I hadn't visited Ravenna on the way down. Once the western capital of the Byzantine world, it would have to wait for another time. Or perhaps as a stop on the way back. I had no plans for this journey. But I knew that I had to take this opportunity to stay away from the temptress that is Italy. The place I always feel so at home. If this trip was to be at all exciting, I would have to get out of Italy. Places like Ravenna – that I could fly to for long weekends – were off la lista.

I met some nice people over a few whiskies at a restaurant near my room and then retired for a rose-coloured and dream-filled sleep.

6

NIGHT BOAT TO PATRAS

The next morning, I wound my way to the top of Ancona's Guasco Hill to visit the cathedral. San Ciriaco – the saint's body is in the crypt apparently – is an impressive and fairly squat building decorated in marble. Very beautiful. I was instantly reminded of St Paul's in London, which although large always appears at a low and human level.

I parked the car directly opposite the steps and took in the views over the harbour. This was a busy and business-like port. Organised and clean-looking with blue cranes and stuccoed cream-coloured harbour offices giving it some style. There was Trajan's gateway, the triumphal arch of crumbly stone against a background of colourful shipping containers. To the left the Lazaretto, a pentagonal low building on its own artificial island, which had acted as a customs shed and quarantine holding. The word quarantine – which comes from the Italian word for forty (quaranta) – was a vital restriction to keep out the plague in older times. New arrivals were held for forty days in the lazaretto to ensure they were clear to enter.

CATTEDRALE DI SAN CIRIACO, ANCONA

I turned back towards the church. The basilica had broad steps and a large entrance flanked by lions carved in pinkish stone. Above this was a round window set in a Romanesque façade. But I guessed this building was not quite as old as that. I was too close to see the famous roof.

The dome of San Ciriaco is not large by modern standards but predates many of the famous medieval ones. A twelve-sided drum supports the dome which had been a wonder in its day before the likes of Brunelleschi created the shock and awe of il Duomo in Florence.

Up here it was overcast and humid with rain in the strong breeze. I entered the church, which was holding a service. The priest was giving a sermon, so I had to tiptoe around. A shame because I had read there was a Bellini and a Piero della Francesca amongst its wonders.

Feeling a bit of an interloper amongst the congregation I left and walked out into the well-kept grounds. Neat, low hedging and raked gravel pathways led to other ancillary buildings. There was a very fine bronze statue of Pope Paul II, appropriately battling a strong headwind of his own. His robes swirling around him in a vast sheet of verdigris dimpled metal. I took a snap of it and said a few words – in both English and Italian – to a Japanese tourist. But she just stared back at me without expression.

◆•▶

Down at the port our boat was in. A big one. We queued with the truck drivers to register our documents. I was nearing the front of the queue when a uniformed guard came up and shouted right in my face. He was obviously furious about something and I shrank back as his spittle hit my cheeks. I made out eventually that he was asking if I was the owner of a red Panda and showed me a scrap of paper with Pedro's number plate on it. I said I was and the rest of the drivers looked sympathetically as he pulled me away and out the doors.

Outside, in the near empty lot, the reason for his agitation was made clear. I had parked in the spot reserved for the fire brigade. Unlucky for me as the rest of the car park was empty. I moved the car to the bay next door and ignored him as he glared at me re-entering the customs shed. Back inside the truck driver who'd been behind me had held my space.

'That guy is well-known round here as an arsehole,' he said.

Papers in order, we went back to the boat. Pedro went down and down, way below the waterline. I pushed his mirrors in and went up and up to deck ten and my cabin. Like being in a floating block of flats.

I walked around and got myself a beer from the open air bar. The decks were painted a lurid turquoise which contrasted with the view. A grey sky with a darker grey sea, putting me in mind of works by Anselm Kiefer. I climbed a staircase and came across a miniature swimming pool on the rear deck. It was empty and covered by an orange safety net. Two kids were using it as a trampoline.

As we set off, we had fine views over Ancona and its elbow-shaped headland. A pleasing panorama of flat-fronted buildings in yellow, beige and ochre colours with here and there one of salmon pink. All very pleasing on the eye. I vowed to return.

◆•▶

I met Rudi and Susan from Munich who had introduced themselves while we waited in the queue at the dock. They were in an ancient camper van that had just had its 400-thousand-kilometre service. Off to the Peloponnese, they were getting off before me at Igoumenitsa. She was originally from Manchester, her German father had met her mother in Austria in the early 1950s and had moved to Britain which I thought must have been awkward so soon after the war. But by the time she was four they were back in Munich. Rudi berated me with moans about all and sundry in the German government. They were off to the self-service restaurant. Would I join them? I said I had to consider la Bella Figura.

Rudi said 'In Germany we have an expression: I don't worry about a bikini body. Because I always sunbathe naked.'

I stayed on the rail, but it started to rain so I crossed through doors to the port side where I would be sheltered in the lee. I leant on the rail and directly below me was the pilot boat very closely alongside. Looking down as it neared closer to the side of the ferry, I saw the pilot step deftly onto the deck from a door many decks below. He gave a wave to the officer on the bridge wing. I gave him a wave too and he threw back a double thumbs up. He was nimble, bearded and with an impressive head of long curly hair. He looked like a poet and not for the first time in Italy I envied the kind of job that entailed.

From bus drivers in Venice to ferry captains in the Bay of Naples, the worthiness and prestige that goes with that open air life was one to covet.

The pilot boat peeled away and I watched it as it went to meet a slowing cargo ship. An elegant design that could only be of Italian origin with containers stacked on deck. Then the rain really started to come down, so I rethought the offer of the self-service restaurant.

◆•▶

The next morning, I was woken at six-thirty by passengers disembarking at Igoumenitsa. It was another eight hours before we would reach our destination, Patras.

Tossing and turning in my bunk I couldn't get back to sleep. I tottered to the bathroom and took a look at myself in the mirror by the light of the fluorescent strip. Not good. I turned off the light while I brushed my teeth.

Last night's pork fillet was not sitting well inside me. Out of boredom – and the rain – I had indeed succumbed to the self-service restaurant. I'd opted for the pork loin but should have settled for a Greek salad.

Truck drivers – who had their own section – were tucking into giant plates of carbs. One guy had rice, pasta and chips which he then spent a minute or two mixing together with a yellow sauce dispensed from the plunger of a five-litre can. I'd taken it for mustard and had squirted some onto my pork only to find out it was some kind of honey dressing.

Later I had retired to the lounge for a beer. When I got to my table, I saw that the barman had charged me 39 euros, ten times too much. Back at the bar he had been replaced by a girl. I questioned the bill, and she took a strand of her hair and pinched it between her nose and upper lip to make a moustache then crossed her eyes at me. I wondered if she was a bit simple. Then the barman appeared again and set off a process of refunding me which required the presence of the first officer and the purser. By the time I got back to my table the girl had cleared my beer away. I chased after her, but she ducked into a doorway and vanished.

7
LOUTAKIA

Morning on the boat deck was fresher with clouds replaced by a sunshiny haze. The sea a true ultramarine and rugged little islands off the beam about two miles distant. There was land on both sides now as we moved due east along the Gulf of Patras.

The ship's tannoy squawked on and chimed, bin, ban bon. It announced in six languages that the self-service restaurant would shortly be opening for lunch. I thought I'd give it a major swerve although – thankfully – the queasiness was retreating.

The fresh air and light on deck was lovely. This was a mid-deck so I was sheltered from the sun, now high in the sky. I opened a watertight door where I'd seen a crewman stowing chairs and pulled one out, dusted it off and sat facing the sea, the breeze and the slowly passing scenery.

I thought of Homer and his 'wine dark sea'. The sea was indeed dark but a rich blue. Flying fish broke the surface and skimmed downwind over the wavelets, obviously avoiding something nasty below.

LOUTAKIA

THE RESTAURANT'S UNGRATEFUL CAT

Then gulls started to appear and held steady in the ship's slipstream. Expert fliers, they'd dip to sea level by spilling the air from their wings and then rise up again to my height without effort. I assumed that their appearance meant we were closing on our destination, but I couldn't see directly forward from my position.

About 20 minutes later the announcement came for all drivers to return to their vehicles.

◆•▸

Reminder to self. Remember the deck number you left your car on. I spent fifteen minutes with the backpack sweating it up and down narrow companionways with everyone else going the other way. I finally found the car, exactly where I had left him. Now, at last we could get off this boat. Twenty-nine hours at sea was getting long.

Patras, and now I was in Greece. After only four days journeying. This had always been my plan. To get as far east as soon as I could. To do so I had booked two ferries. The one I was disembarking, from Ancona to Patras, and the other from Piraeus – in Athens – to Chios, a small Greek island just off the coast of Turkey.

I followed the traffic out of the port assuming they knew their way. It was a vast apron of concrete with not a sign to be seen. Out and onto the road. Still no customs or passport check. So, once you were in the EU that was it? Despite being from a 'third country'?

The coast road was brand new and sort of finished. One of those high spec European jobs and fairly empty.

The drivers, so different from the Italians. Respectful in that kind of disinterested way. Pedro and I bowled along at 130 kmh. All the windows down and the smell of wild thyme and rosemary flooding the nostrils. It was quite windy and the flapping seat belts made even more noise than usual. I'd been wearing T-shirts and my arm out the window meant that I was getting quite the farmer's tan. Starboard out and starboard home was the only way with a right-hand drive car.

I went 20 klicks in the wrong direction when the satnav got confused. There were no junctions to turn off at. I had realised pretty quickly because the sea was on the wrong side and coming to a section of the motorway without a crash barrier we did a sneaky U-turn across the eight lanes of both carriageways. There was nobody about really. I thought to myself, what it would take to allow such a manoeuvre on the M25.

We followed the coast round and in the late afternoon we reached Loutakia. An eye-pleasing bay on the road just beyond Corinth. Pretty rough and ready on the roadside with cars parked higgledy-piggledy on the dusty verge, and of ages that made Pedro seem a youngster.

This is the sort of place I always like to stay but you would never find it online. It was hardly even on the map. It had a touch of the Wild West about it. And a feeling of opportunity with its lack of gentrification.

I checked into the first hotel I came to. A nice place with a garden that led down to a private beach and all for just 32 euros a night.

Then sauntered down to the Anykoniades restaurant and ordered a Fix, sitting like Shirley Valentine in a bent-wood chair on the pebbly beach with my toes in the water.

I had a boat booked from Piraeus in two days time and had flirted with the idea of staying in Athens to do the sights. But it was too hot, the crowds would be too big. I binned that thought. The wonders of the Parthenon would have to wait for another day. I'd no doubt get my fill of archaeology in Turkey. And that wasn't what this trip was about, really. Why put yourself through the hassle just for the bragging rights of having been there and done that? This was something that yoga had taught me. The beauty of JOMO.

It was 5pm in the restaurant and under the beach awning two old dowagers were drinking ouzo and picking through some fried fish, eating with cigarettes in their mouths. They'd ordered massive platefuls. A bored factotum, bug-eyed and looking a little like Peter Lorre, was chain-smoking Marlboro reds and sitting at the end of their table. Their driver I imagined. After an hour they creaked off leaving untouched the Nescafe they'd just ordered.

Meanwhile, in front of me, a father and his two young daughters were shrieking and giggling as they entered the water. It took them nearly half an hour to get in. But once they had he couldn't get those two water babies out again. He'd made the error of getting out first expecting them to follow and now he was dry and dressed he couldn't go back in and catch them. They teased him for 20 minutes before relenting.

Later that night, after a doze in air-conditioned comfort, I went out for a chat and a snifter. There were no streetlamps so I made my way by the light of the stars. On my way back back, in the almost pitch blackness I stepped off the pavement and into thin air. The unguarded drop off was only about four feet but I put out my arms and whacked my elbow on the top of the wall. The Wild West held its dangers as strongly as its opportunities.

◆•▶

On the second night I had a brilliant fish soup made with grouper. The restaurant's cat could obviously smell it and sat by my chair making a racket. But when I offered him a bit on a piece of bread, he turned his nose up and sidled off. How rude!

8

TO PIRAEUS

Next morning, the sun rose on the Saronic Gulf. A blinding white ball set in an orange sky. The sea was stained sepia by contrast, and on it, as if lit by a searchlight, a small white and blue fishing boat puttering out to sea.

By the time I'd finished 15 minutes of stretching, the sun was high in the sky and hot. I'd felt it burning my tootsies as I lay on the floor and had to shut the black-out curtains. The sky once again blue. Another scorcher today then.

On the horizon were the two small islands of Agios Ionnis and Agios Thomas and behind them I knew was Aegina.

I'd been to Aegina when I teamed up with an art director to work at a sales conference in Athens. We had both thought it too good an opportunity to miss visiting an island on expenses. So, we flew out two days earlier and took the first boat from Piraeus to the first island we came to. That turned out to be Aegina. The port was a bit touristy, so we jumped in a cab and asked the driver to take us to a good restaurant with rooms.

TO PIRAEUS

The very beautiful bay with crystal water he dropped us at was where I'd had the best Greek salad of my life. That was twenty years ago now, but I often wonder if it's all still there and untouched. Or even if I could find it again.

◆•▶

DAWN OVER THE SARONIC ISLANDS

Today I had some time to kill. I didn't have to get to the port until six, so I rearranged the chaos of the car boot. Separating clothes for washing, etc.

The ferry from Piraeus that night was taking me to the Greek island of Chios, a few miles off the Turkish coast near Izmir. I'd first heard of it watching Michael Wood's TV series on the Trojan War. Every time he had mentioned it he had called it 'lovely Chios' and it certainly did look gorgeous on screen. That had put the hook in me, and I'd bitten down hard.

With a family and a wife with a very important job, it's really hard to get away for more than ten days. You certainly don't want to spend two of those days travelling. But now I did have the time and once this ferry ride was over, no plan to do anything other than get into Turkey and eventually find my way home.

◆•▶

Down at breakfast, the man who always ate with his mouth open had his back to me. I'd tried to ignore his cement mixer mastication yesterday. Patience and acceptance, whispered the shoulder on my guru side. On the other shoulder a voice said to go and get the gaffer tape from Pedro's boot.

The temperature on the terrace was very pleasant and a slight breeze cooled my knees. I had my usual pint of coffee and four glasses of iced water as I wandered over the lawn and down to the water of the hotel's tiny private beach.

I checked out and chatted to the girl on the desk while she insisted on printing me a receipt.

'You were lucky to find us open. We've had so few visitors. We almost closed for the season last week.'

'What will you do in the winter?' I said.

'I really don't know. Work here is very scarce. I may have to go home to my mother who lives in the mountains. But I hope not.'

◆•▶

Just up the road there was a little promontory with a lighthouse. I thought it might make for a pleasant diversion. I found the right turning and we dropped down through lanes between houses to the sea.

It was a Sunday and on a scrappy bit of beach, families were already getting settled in for the day. I hoped they'd all been to church.

I drove on. The concrete ran out, but I kept going, protecting my tyres as best I could. I could hear a tinkling sound from the left. What could that be? Before I got out to investigate, I realised it was the knife and fork I'd pinched from the ferry and put in the glove box.

Rounding a bend, I was confronted by a banked-up earthwork. A cliff fall had taken out the track. Ah well, the lighthouse would keep. I reversed up all the way to the black top and continued my journey, tyres ticking with gravel.

Suddenly, a blue light big in the mirror. The cop was very close to my bumper. I had the usual heart in the throat moment but it was just a convoy of local bigwigs. They swooshed by in unison once the road straightened out.

After a bit we came into Isthmus. One of the two

bridges over the Corinth Canal. I'd seen pictures of it – and as a kid, once had a jigsaw of a ship passing through it – but was not prepared for how spectacular it is when you're there. I was amazed by its depth and narrowness. The limestone cliffs were sheer and at the bottom – far below – the canal, a chalky teal blue. Incredible that this had been dug by hand. It was straight as a die.

The canal has a chequered history. Despite massive attempts in ancient times, it was only completed in 1893, having bankrupted several consortia in the process. Its narrowness means that big ships can't use it and it funnels the wind to make navigation difficult. Added to that, the two seas it links have differing tide times, which creates a very strong current as one side flows into the other and vice versa. Its lack of commercial success is matched by just how spectacular it is to behold.

We drove on, and with plenty of time to spare, took the coast road. The sea was mostly at the bottom of a hundred-foot cliff along this stretch of coast. Anywhere there was any possibility of parking, a car was plonked in the gap. Almost with wheels overhanging the bluffs. I stopped and watched one family struggling down the near vertical limestone, clinging to scrub to prevent themselves from falling.

We came into Athens' outskirts. Here they had put in two miles of eight-lane highway before you were dumped into the narrows of Athens' streets. A Lamborghini flashed up behind me and whipped past with a plangent howl. Now and again, there were good views of the Parthenon.

Down in the giant port of Piraeus I went round and around trying to find my dock gate but always winding up sitting at the same set of lights. Pedro was waved at by three old men sitting in a street cafe as we came back for the third time. I stopped to ask the way, but they didn't understand and offered me ouzo with toothless grins. A friendly taxi driver came over and got me straight. It meant driving back out of town and taking an unmarked filter that I'd passed on the way in.

I found my boat but was way too early to board. I left Pedders on the blistering dock and sat on a bench in the shade of a lime tree. The view was of the harbour entrance. So much activity. Everywhere you looked ships, hydrofoils and catamaran ferries were leaving or docking. A blue hydrofoil, exactly the same as the one we had taken to Aegina, throbbed past low in the water, its aluminium panels looking grey and beaten. I wondered if it was the same one.

A derelict building had been clad with an enormous poster celebrating the battle of Salamis. Bloody hell! That was 2,500 years ago. It put the military ports of Plymouth and Portsmouth with our naval history in perspective. What must this natural harbour have been like here at the height of classical Athens' power?

WAITING TO LOAD IN PIRAEUS

9

NEA MONI

Two-thirty in the am, I was woken by a loud banging on my cabin door.

'Yes… yes?' I managed to stumble out.

'Meester waking up please! Ship is docking!'

Chios, widely believed to be the birthplace of Homer, I'm not loving you right now.

On deck hundreds of young men were yawning and looking sorry for themselves. Among them – somewhere – were George, George, George and Jason. And probably a few more Georges too. I'd met these four lads the evening before and stood them a couple of rounds. They were on their way to start their nine months of national service. The army has a large training camp on the island.

Off the ship we pulled to one side and let the ferry traffic go. Lorry after lorry knew their way and disappeared into the night. I put the car into gear, and we drove away from the dock in the pitch black. Up and up the hillside, round and round the hairpins towards Nea Moni, the monastery in the mountainous centre of the island. This was one of the places I'd come to see so

I thought we might as well aim for it. Nowhere was open yet and no rooms were to be had at this hour anyway.

It was a clear night but country dark. Pedro's headlamps, which have the candlepower of just one candle, were even more useless with the beam deflectors on. I took my time, nose on the windscreen. Groping like a blinking mole for a sudden drop-off that might send us both to the bottom of a gorge.

Nearing the monastery, I spotted a generous lay-by set into the pines and boulders. I parked up rather than wake the monks. It was a lovely night and cool-ish. I considered sleeping on the ground but, inspecting it with a torch I found it was covered with small rocks and particularly vicious thistles, so I wound down the seat and popped my coat under my head. It was eerily quiet, in the distance the faint tinkle of a goat's bell. On the point of dropping off I heard soft footsteps approaching. I laid low but they didn't stop. Who could be walking around at this hour? The stranger was probably thinking something similar of me.

Later, the wind got up and the trees were creaking and swaying above me. I got out to a ceiling of brilliant stars. Then, biffo! My upturned face was hit by a small branch that had fallen from one of the pines, I retreated back to the car. The roof and bonnet bonged as pine cones bounced off, taking away more of Pedro's paint lacquer. It had become chilly, so I unfolded the quilt and tried to catch a few more zeds.

◆•▶

In the morning, I got out and stretched. There was a

small track away from the lay-by that I realised now must have been created for several vehicles to park. I followed it and came to a clearing of grass. The boulders (some the size of Pedro) had been moved to form an irregular perimeter wall. In the middle was a substantially made altar, it was too high to be a table. I wondered if I was standing in an open air church.

◆•▶

John Gaskin's excellent book – The Traveller's Guide to Classical Philosophy – waxes in awe of Nea Moni.

'It is far from the madding crowd and almost abandoned by worldly religion, but an aura of peace and ancient holiness lingers there and holds the pilgrim. Go there alone if you can.'

It was 8am. If I had a shot at that solitude, then it was now. I got back to the road and brushed my teeth, then started up the lil' donkey and we rolled down the hill.

The monastery came into view as we rounded a bend and I stopped to take a snap. A magical setting with cypresses and olives and the boulder-strewn landscape sharpened by the creamy blue sky in the background.

As I took the photo a woman in a tiny car (even tinier than Peds) passed and waved. She turned out to be the curator and by the time we arrived she had opened up and was sitting with an iced coffee.

I walked in through the main gate. On the left was a small building that housed an ossuary of sorts with previous monks' skulls piled up in glass-fronted bookcases, their femurs bundled together on the bottom shelf. The woman was feeding a motley crew of stray cats.

NEA MONI

*GONE BUT NOT FORGOTTEN.
BONES OF MONKS AT NEA MONI MONASTERY.*

What a wondrous place it is. Three local prophets had foretold that Constantine – then in exile on Lesbos – would come to great power. That turned out to be a good call on their part because when Byzantium became Constantinople these seers were rewarded by patronage and the founding of a monastery – Nea Moni – in 1120.

A large priest in orthodox garb and tricorn hat emerged from a tiny house and beckoned me over to the church which he unlocked with an ancient key. Inside it was extraordinary, with Byzantine mosaics and all kinds of arcane religious paraphernalia. I thought how much G would have loved it. A twinge of deep fondness for my wife of 27 years.

In a shell-lined niche I lit a candle to Elizabeth II, whose funeral was taking place in London later that day.

I walked around the outside of the church and explored the ruins which were in an abandoned state of archaeological investigation. I guessed they'd run out of money.

The views were pleasant over the wooded hills in this remote part of the island, and I spent some time in the partial shade of a fig tree to take it all in.

Nea Moni – which means New Monastery – is also famous for being the site of a tragedy. In 1822, thousands of Greek villagers had gathered here to shelter from the advancing Ottoman troops during the Greek War of Independence. The Turks' actions had meant the flight, death or enslavement of more than four-fifths of the island's population, already swollen with refugees from neighbouring islands. Around 25 thousand were killed. Fearing the worst, the local villagers threw themselves from the monastery's cliffs rather than be captured. I peered down through the rising trees to the rocks below and tried to imagine it.

◆•▶

In the late afternoon I visited Mesta. One of the fortified villages that had been responsible for the mastic gum trade. These mastic trees only grow in Chios and its gum is made into a chewable confectionery that was much prized by the Ottoman Turks who lavished those who produced it. Evidenced by Mesta's spectacularly ornate village church. The Sultan had protected the trade and had effectively imprisoned the producers in these heavily fortified towns. Stealing mastic was punishable by death. The Ottoman equivalent of poaching Henry VIII's deer.

I had a mastic ice cream. A very difficult flavour to describe. And certainly not available from your local builders' merchant.

On the way back to my room at the harbour we detoured to Apostika. A narrow and single-track road which contoured the hills and provided terrific views over the mastic terraces and olive groves.

The beach at the end was deserted and the water lovely. Gin clear and just as refreshing. As I was drying off, a couple I'd seen in the village arrived for a dip. They'd obviously spotted my car.

'You from London?' the man asked. The couple were German. 'I have a sister who lives there. Next to Harrods.'

I suggested that must be very convenient. We chatted for a bit and they said they had fully explored the island.

'Have you been to Nea Moni?' I asked.

They hadn't and I told them a little about it, before trudging up the shingle.

'Hey!' he shouted, and I turned.

'God save the King!' he said. 'God save the King.' I replied, thinking what a strange thing for a German to say.

When I got to the car, I tore the monastery's page from my guidebook and put it under their wiper blade.

10

CHIOS TOWN

The Hotel Kyma sits on a tiny promontory overlooking the Turkish coast and the harbour of Chios Town. Small, but with the faded grandeur of a much bigger establishment. Its considerable charm is matched only by the owner Theodore and his lovely wife Guher. He is Greek and she a Turk, which makes for a powerful combination, and one that's hard to resist.

I had been fretting that I couldn't get my car booked on a ferry, across the straits to Cesme on the Turkish side. I said that I was going up to the port to try to sort it out.

'No, don't do that,' said Theo. 'Have a coffee in the lounge and I will make enquiries for you.'

I wandered to the terrace beyond the lounge and sat outside in the sunshine.

There was a considerable wind blowing – the Meltemi – a northerly. It belied the heat of the day and made it a very refreshing place to ponder and watch the ships going in and out of the harbour.

After a bit Guher returned with the phone and said that the earliest boat with availability was at six pm

CHIOS TOWN

A SHIP APPROACHING CHIOS HARBOUR

tomorrow. I agreed that was fine and she suggested that I pick the tickets up soon just in case.

Finding the Turyol office, I presented all the relevant documents and returned.

'All okay?' asked Theodore, I nodded my thanks.

'Good, good. Did they ask if the car was in your name?'

'Yes they did.'

The logbook was in my name, but it was not something that I had thought about.

'A month ago, this couple stayed with us and left for Turkey,' he said. 'When they arrived, they said the port authority had examined their documents and found that the car was in a company name. This meant they were made to go to the regional capital to sort out the paperwork, taking the best part of a day. I only found this out because they told me all about it on their way back.'

Phew, I thought. No matter how much you research, you still have to learn on the ground.

◆•▶

I sauntered through the town to a restaurant they'd recommended north of the port. I was told to avoid the castle, which blocked off the coast. But after an hour I was completely lost. My middle toe on my right foot – which had been dogging me most of the trip – was now throbbing and making me limp badly.

Coming to a tyre-fitters I went in to ask for directions. I was immediately taken to a woman sitting in isolated splendour in a soundproofed and air-conditioned office at the back of the shop. She brought me a cup of coffee and called a cab.

'You are completely in the wrong part of town. It is a 40-minute walk from here and at midday you will fry.'

We got chatting and I told her that I had driven from London.

'Oh!' she said, smiling, 'I don't suppose you need any tyres?' I laughed.' 'I had to ask,' she said, 'my boss would beat me if I didn't!'

The cab dropped me at a concrete pier. Big fishing boats moored alongside and tables set out around the building with blue and white tablecloths flapping in the breeze. This is the simple welcome that you see everywhere you go in this country. Signifying the promise of good food and great hospitality.

On the way the driver had said that it was a very good place for fresh fish. Make sure you drink ouzo with it, it goes very well with seafood. I told him my ouzo drinking days were behind me.

'If you don't drink ouzo, I'm not picking you up again!'

'Okay, okay… I'll give it a shot.' Easily led, this boy.

The restaurant was no more than the kitchen of a house attached to the fish market, which was all over for the day. Outside, two fishermen had just finished a plate of fried shrimps, so I ordered the same with a bottle of ouzo and a beer. They were fantastic and yes, I truly believe their flavour was enhanced by the ouzo. Ahem..!

The waitress came and cleared the fishermen's table by folding all the remains onto the paper tablecloth. Immediately, 20 or so very skinny cats arrived from nowhere and followed her around the building for their midday feast.

Nearing the end of service, the waitress clocked off and walked out to her car giving me a wave. I was the only customer left. A black and white cat – obviously her favourite – walked on its hind legs alongside her as she stroked its head. It jumped through the window into her car as she started up. She got out and removed it from the passenger seat and it ran around and got in the driver's door. After seeing her remove it twice more I went over to help her and picked up the cat, waving his paw at her disappearing car.

When the cab arrived, he blew his horn at me. I had been dozing with my head against the sunny wall. He sat with the engine running and the doors locked until I walked back to the table and showed him the empty ouzo bottle.

'Okay then, let's go,' he said with a grin.

Back at the hotel I stumbled up the impressive marble staircase to my room. I opened the shutters which looked original and were rounded by thousands of coats of paint against the sea breeze. Outside on the generous balcony I sat in a chair and tried to read. But the gentle warmth and soothing zephyrs and of course, the bloody ouzo, had made me sleepy. So, I got into bed, under sheets so heavily starched that I had to pat them down around me.

Falling asleep with the doors open and the muslin curtain wafting in the breeze I was reminded of Tennyson's The Lotos-Eaters:

In the afternoon they came unto a land
In which it seemed always afternoon.

CHIOS TOWN

All round the coast the languid air did swoon,
Breathing like one that hath a weary dream.

◆•▶

Next morning, my toe, which I examined in the bathroom, was swollen into an angry red comma. I wondered if I had broken it. I thought I'd better get it looked at by a medic at some point.

The bath was one of those plastic corner-shaped jacuzzi things and took up most of the room. It creaked worryingly as I stood in it to shower. I tried to keep the water from going down the sides which were not attached to the wall. I thought how ironic this was on an island famed for its mastic production.

It was getting steamy. There was a small window at head height, with a moving shadow behind it that I took for a piece of litter. As I unlatched it, in rushed a great flurry of grey, downy feathers that stuck all over my wet body. I looked down. I was completely feathered. As I looked up, staring back at me was a slim pigeon. It had a curious look on its face as it cocked its head to and fro. I slammed the window before it could join me in the bath for its morning ablutions. I rinsed off and unplugged the drain. Big sigh.

I had a pleasant breakfast of soft-boiled eggs, toast and coffee and asked Theodore if I could negotiate a late check-out.

'No need,' he said, 'the room is yours gratis. Stay until your boat sails.'

I asked him for an envelope. I wanted to post back the key to the room I'd stayed in the night before which I had forgotten to return.

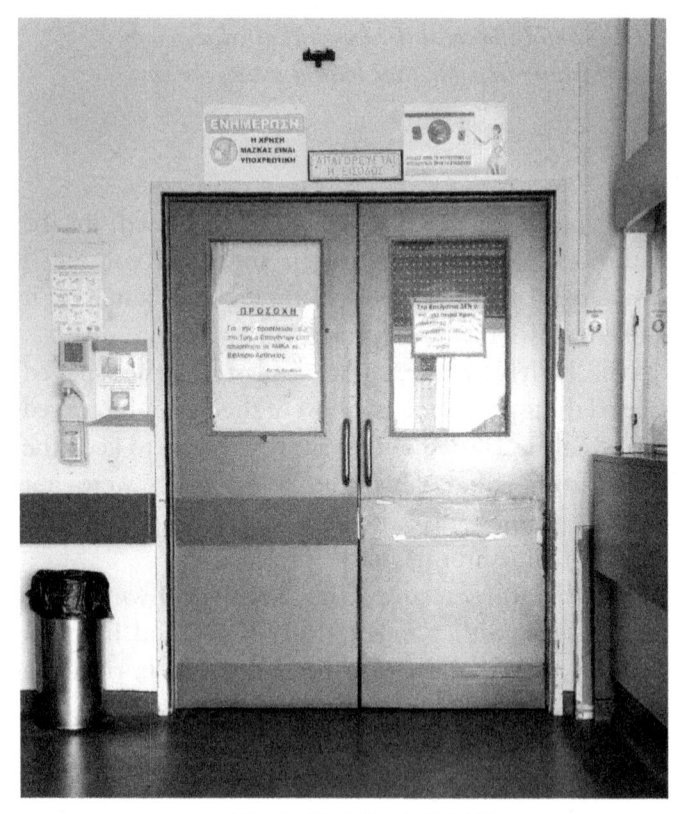

ED ENTRANCE, CHIOS HOSPITAL

'Don't worry about that. We have an excursion going to Mesta tomorrow and I'll get them to drop it off.'

A highly resourceful man then, and a problem solver.

Noticing my limp Theo suggested I went to get it checked out. I thought, well why not? I had all day.

Finding the hospital was no problem and I parked up in front of A&E. You couldn't do that at home.

Inside there were people lying around on trolleys in various states of disrepair.

They'd put me in a wheelchair in front of a sad-looking boy who'd obviously taken a face plant in his school playground. His tongue continuously investigating the place where his front teeth had once resided.

The doctor hemmed and hawed over my toe and the nurse came over to take some blood. Then I was wheeled up to x-ray. So far, so good. They parked me in front of a window worthy of any architect where I could look out at the ocean. I watched tankers and ferries pass, which was interesting at first. But there I stayed for the next six hours. At this point I was seriously considering cancelling my ferry that evening. In the nick of time the doctor turned up, drew up a stool and went through my results on an impressive piece of paper. All in Greek, naturally. But the gist was no bones broken. Not gout either, although he couldn't rule it out. In truth he wasn't sure what the problem was. I got a prescription for antibiotics and anti-inflammatories, and I hopped it – literally – to the car before the pharmacies closed. Today was early closing. Who knew?

Back at the hotel, Theodore was charming as ever. Refused to take a penny for the beers I'd had the night before and undercharged me for the room. When I pressed him, he pushed the money away.

'Mr Nic, you have already suffered enough today.'

Thanking him I hotfooted it – again literally – to the port.

11

SIREN CALL

Now I was in Turkey.

The ferry – the previous evening – had been comfortable despite quite a big sea running. It was a short trip and most of the passengers sat up on deck. I got talking to some tipsy Turkish couples who'd been over to Chios on a day trip.

Among the few cars onboard there was a baby blue Bentley with Ukranian plates and a retired German couple who were driving a converted – and massive – fire truck to Tehran in Iran.

'We're a bit worried about the bit through Iraq,' the wife told me.

Coming across from Chios into Cesme on the Turkish coast it became clear that the flag manufacturers were having a boom time. They are everywhere here. Even on lamp posts. And a massive banner on top of the hill above the town.

We were approaching the dock and the confused waters were making the ferry lurch and roll. Looking down on the car deck I saw several foot-passengers holding onto Pedro's roof rails. You see G? That's what you need a roof rack for.

Queues for immigration, then for customs, where chassis numbers and dates of manufacture for Pedro were entered into a database, probably never to be seen again. Green card inspected. Passport stamped both for me and for him. And then I was finally, after two hours, through customs. But the car was still inside the dock. I went back in and through the now unguarded immigration gates to rescue him. Finally, I found the way out, but the main gates could not be opened until a special guard returned from the toilet, another twenty minutes.

When at last he turned up, he said,

'Got anything in the trunk?'

I said yes, thinking here we go, a long day already, about to get longer.

But he said, 'Okay then, you can go,' and whistled to the soldier to open the gate. He'd probably had a long day too.

◆•▶

The hotel that Guher had booked me into was a business travellers' place. It was cubic. Everything was on a massive scale and square. The atrium was a football field by a football field by a football field in dimensions. The furniture was square, my bed was square, even the tooth glass in the bathroom was square. I thought, I'm in a Minecraft nightmare, I gotta get out.

Outside it was a balmy night. Down the street I found a guy locking up a trike and scooter rental place and asked where I could get a taxi to the port area.

'Hop on,' he said, pointing to his quad bike. 'I'll give you a ride, I'm going that way.'

He dropped me at a very nice steak restaurant. But I was past eating and just had a beer.

This was just one of a string of fairly busy eateries on the promenade with big boats moored stern to. The clientele were well-heeled. I gave up my table when I saw a group of four couldn't get seated and waved away their thanks. When the time came to pay my bill, the waiter said that they had covered it.

◆•◆

In the morning I was blocked in by a double-parked Mercedes. I assumed it was the suited guys sitting at breakfast in the hotel, so I approached their table. They said they were just concluding a deal and would be five minutes. Would I join them? I said I would, and they whistled to the waiter to set another place. While the contracts on the table were being signed, I got chatting to one of them.

'How did you get here?'

'I drove from London in my car. I caught some ferries to get here quickly, and I'll drive slowly back.'

'Interesting, we import cars for clients all the time. You might want to think about that next time?'

I replied that the journey was the thing. But yes, I thought. Wouldn't it be great to fly out and pick up your car from the docks.

◆•◆

THE ROAD OUT OF CESME

Soon after leaving Cesme, you come into a startling landscape reminiscent of those I had seen in movies shot in the desert states of the US. A dead straight and undulating road disappearing to low hills wobbling in the hazy and mirage-filled distance. Desert-like low scrub at the sides of the road went on for what looked like miles. Not a place to break down.

Ahead, a long way up the road, a couple of large trucks pulled out in front of me. They'd come out of a cement works and were trailing clouds of white dust that I could barely see through. I had to get past them, but they were really motoring. I spent quite a long time on the wrong side of the road bouncing around on the rough and narrow tarmac. We were all doing about 80 mph. Then I got past and into clean air. They blew their air horns at us, and Pedro tooted back.

After a while, we started to approach Izmir, the local capital. The outskirts are filled with heavy industry and a great deal of pollution. Even the vanes of the wind turbines are coated and stained brown. The smells were not great either. I was taken back to my chemistry class. Ammonia, toluene, butyric acid – which smells like vomit – but mostly the smell of burning rubber. All very nasty.

Izmir had once been a pleasant town. But its demise began after the First World War when the Greeks invaded and set fire to the waterfront buildings. The ensuing ethnic violence enacted by Greek troops strengthened Turkish nationalism, ensuring the final nail in the coffin of the Ottoman Empire.

Next we came to some of the biggest office buildings I had ever seen. They looked like university or research buildings, but I couldn't be sure. The scale was enormous. Gargantuan and all built, along with hundreds of residential blocks, on steep hillsides.

The road itself, even though I had opted to drive off the main highway, was now four-lane carriageways and a massive engineering feat. They had moved mountains – literally – to keep the grade shallow. It was road-building on an epic scale, and I wondered why it was all really needed.

◆•◆

I had planned on staying at Eski Foca. Its jagged black rocks that, when the Meltemi blows, make a howling whine said to be that of the sirens of mythology. Odysseus had his crew tie him to the mast to resist them as he sailed past on his way home. But the road was closed and I wound up in the pleasant little fishing village of Yeni Foca, its sister to the north.

Yeni Foca was full of small fishing boats. It was sunny but cold in the wind and none of the outside restaurants were taking any custom. It must be quite a

SIREN CALL

FIRE CONTROL HELICOPTER LOADING WATER

sight in the summer months, crowded out with – mostly local – visitors.

In the back lanes I found a hole in the wall kebab place and ate on the street.

Reaching my room, a loud clattering from outside. A big helicopter was filling up a giant bucket from the harbour. It was then followed by another helicopter. This went on for much of the afternoon. Obviously, a fire somewhere needed putting out.

Later that evening I wandered around a bit, wearing a fleece. It was very windy and only a few stalwarts were braving the weather. There was one restaurant where locals were fighting small bony fish for their flesh. But I couldn't be bothered to sit down to a meal, so I called it a night.

Not for the first time did I ponder that one of the joys of travelling alone is that you can suit yourself.

12

A LITTLE BIT OF TOAST

Breakfast was served in the canvas and glass affair attached to the front of the pansyon. I had some tomato soup. Not my typical morning go-to, but very good indeed.

Outside it was breezy with the onshore wind whipping up wavelets near the promenade and white horses out to sea. Two large mastiffs were patrolling as if they owned the place and giving anyone on foot – or bicycle – a hard time. They were intimidating even to the obvious locals who tried to give them a wide berth.

Back inside the dining tent, a thermostat must have decided that the temperature was too low, and a massive blower attached to the wall started up. It turned what had been a serene and contemplative moment of tinkling cutlery into a comedic farce.

Anything less heavy than a bottle of water was blown up into the air. Butter pats and paper cups of honey blew across the room and one landed in a woman's hair. The staff, instead of turning off the offending heater scurried around corralling paper napkins and flying bits of cake. I made a hasty exit from the chaos onto the prom.

I felt guilty. But in truth I was close to giggling. One ventilator incident after another. Perhaps I was finally getting a fan following?

Outside the sun was shining and the wind was strong. It was a cold northerly and a puffer jacket was definitely in order. I went to pat one of the local guard dogs. But it bared its drooly gums at me and I thought better of it.

Shouldering my bag I walked to the car at the rear. A cat came towards me mewling, then abruptly stopped to defecate in the middle of the road. I treated it as a roundabout and walked on.

◆•◆

The road soon headed inland and away from the coast. Again, the landscapes got big.

From time to time, I was noticing what looked like balled-up Kleenex bouncing around on the road. But it was too light and floaty for that. After a toll booth I caught up a giant lorry. Two storeys high and domed over with a massive tarp. Out the sides little balls of white stuff were appearing and bouncing off my windscreen. I thought it must be that squiggly worm stuff that's used for packing. But later, as the motorway became a dualled road, I started to see cotton growing, so that's what it was! These were small-holdings at first. Then huge acreages of it. Pretty to look at. Then the farms gave way to salt pans. Mauve and translucent blue hues that were very soothing on the eye.

We continued on the dual carriageway but… eyes front! A tractor and trailer crossing. A pair of dogs trotting along the barrier. Then, coming the other way, a horse and cart. The horse rearing at the oncoming traffic.

◆•▶

Next stop, Ayvalik. Not my kind of place really. Nice enough in an old-fashioned kind of way with cobbled streets making everyone walk like drunkards. It was the Turkish coast of my youth. Narrow alleys strung over with vines and coloured lanterns. Windows dressed up with all kinds of painted bric-a-brac. I had found it charming then but a bit kiss-me-quick now. Most of the waterfront had been nabbed by hotels.

It was still a centre for olive oil production. I had seen stalls everywhere along the roads. But the old chimneys of the pressing plants – dotted all over the town – were derelict. Everything happened in big factories now. The olives here are grown in very large numbers. Not like the small collectives you see elsewhere. Wandering to the outskirts I found a little man with a brazier cooking kebabs under a vine-strewn awning and had a beer. I called my parents' home and spoke to Dad, which made me feel guilty. He was struggling with Mum, who was now bed-ridden. He was a little teary and the traffic noise made it hard to have a conversation with him of any seriousness. I told him I'd call back when I was in a quiet place.

Back in the centre I parked up in an Otopark and asked the attendant who was having tea with some

CHEESE SHOP, AYVALIK

other men, if there was anywhere cheap to stay. He sat me down, offered me a glass of chai and sent a text. Almost immediately a young women materialised.

'We go to room now?' she said.

I cocked an eyebrow and followed her next door and up two flights to a cell-like room.

'Hom many night?' she asked.

'Only one,' I replied and she showed me a number on her phone that was the equivalent of six quid. I thumbed over the Turkish and she handed me the key with a little bow.

◆•▸

At night the town calmed from the frenetic, traffic cramped sweat-box it had been during the day.

I called my father back. He never complained but I could tell he really was having a hard time caring for Mum. I felt guilty that I was not there to help him and selfish taking this long trip. But she had been in gradual decline for several years now.

◆•▸

I wasn't particularly hungry but wandered half-heartedly in search of the toast of the town. I'd heard that this place was famous for the ultimate street snack. A toasted sandwich that would definitely hit the spot, hungry or not. The kind of thing Rick Stein would be in raptures about. But it was hard to find. Reaching darkness on the edge of town I approached what I thought was a bus station. Instead, it happened to be toast central. A collection of twelve toast-selling outlets all with their charming girls or pressurising boys.

At ranked tables, at least 500 people were chowing down on this toast. Basically, a kebab – with the works – in two slices of doughy bread that had been heated under a grill.

Most people were opting for the full enchilada. I wandered the identical rows of toast sellers until accosted by Abdullah. The toast looked good. And he was persuasive. But I just couldn't do it. I couldn't sit in a refectory eating a sandwich with all those other people in their coats, bent over and swivelling their heads at other tables? Too much like school dinners. A good Lebanese friend ran a sandwich shop that would beat anything here. I wondered what he would have made of it.

Wandering back, I met a couple from San Diego. He was wearing a bandana and she beads. I took a chance and asked if they were hippies?

'Absolutely!' said Rainey.

You could see her sparkle of youth. She was seventy-five but looked mid-fifties. Evidently, life was agreeing with her.

'Why are you here?' I asked.

'Well, our dog died.'

I commiserated.

'Yah, well, so then we had no ties and we decided to take a two-year trip. He's from Istanbul.' She said, pointing at her partner.

I didn't get his name, but he too was charming. Slightly grizzled in an Iggy Pop kind of way. He'd come back from LA to see a sick sister-in-law and had been called up to do national service when he arrived. He'd been dodging that in California for decades.

'They made me do four months in the "Grandad Regiment", not so bad.'

I asked what he had done for work. He'd been a chef, or at least worked in a restaurant. 'People used to ask me – when they found out I was from Stanbul – how we prepared the food. I'd always told 'em it was outtakan. "Ottoman?" they'd say. No! Out a can!'

I laughed and they got up to leave.

'By the way,' Rainey said. 'This looks like an innocent place but, if anyone invites you to a party, don't go.'

Behind her Iggy Pop nodded and gave the thumbs down. Then they were gone.

I was kind of shocked and thought for a while about what they had meant.

I went the other way down the street. Jackdaws were roosting noisily and clattering about in their usual gregarious way in the trees. I stepped out into the road to avoid their droppings.

Later I found a pleasant wine bar. A large fella was singing traditional songs. A kind of one-man band with guitar, bells on one foot and something like a tabla on the other. Not my kind of thing normally but his singing was so impassioned that I stayed for two hours.

13

INTO GREAT BEAUTY

I had to admit that my travels from the bay of Izmir northwards had not exactly wowed me. Too much industry and sprawling, ugly towns had left me a little in need of some natural beauty.

At Edremit, where the coast turns westward, the road gave out to a single track. They were still building the rest of the highway and now and then you could see the tunnels and bridges they had completed and were yet to join up.

JETTY, SIVRICE WITH LESBOS IN THE DISTANCE

I was going to a motel that had been recommended by a hotel owner I had contacted in Assos. I had wanted to stay with her but she was closed.

'Do you need to be downtown in Assos?' she said. 'If not, you might like to experience something like a motel I know in Sivrice. Then you can do an early morning visit on Sunday to Assos when everybody is asleep. It's not luxury but unique, they don't speak English but it's a perfect spot to experience the local environment, people and food.'

'Sounds great,' I said.

'Be sure to be taking your bathing suit.'

I had not quite reckoned on what it might be like but was confronted with a place of great charm and stunning views over the neighbouring Greek island of Lesbos.

This, I was told, was the short stretch of water that every day had seen boats laden with migrants cross to the island. They were getting out of Turkey and into Greece and the EU. It had all stopped now. A combination of a clampdown by the Turkish authorities aided by EU funding had pinched out this route. I wondered grimly how they had made that happen and was told that some force was used including removing the migrants' outboards and setting them adrift. After a while the people smugglers moved on. I remembered the terrible images of dead children being carried off the beaches while tourists sunbathed nearby that had really put Lesbos on the map. And for all the wrong reasons. The camp on the island was still there. What now for those people?

◆◆◆

YOU'LL NEVER DINE ALONE

I had appreciated the run in as the road toiled upwards and the country got wilder. Truly beautiful mountainous countryside, I was all alone here. The traffic I had been following had found an easier route.

The country was pretty and green. I came to a crossroads with a tea house and a couple of men playing backgammon in the shade. I stopped and ordered some chai, checking Pedro's water while I waited and filling up the washer bottle from a spout in the wall.

Then later I came to a small hamlet, circling a stagnant and bright green pond. That was the highest point. Then steeply downhill on a very rough road, petering out to sand and the entrance to the motel.

What a spot. A rough car park by the sea and behind it a collection of homemade sheds which were the rooms. Spotless inside with crisp white sheets and a tiny bathroom. I dropped off my bag and wandered to a lean-to with a few tables and chairs which made up the restaurant.

You used to be able to find this sort of thing all along the Turkish coast, but tourism was now big business. The dreaded 'all inclusive' had replaced this tranquillity with jet skis and banana boats.

There were two young couples down from Istanbul for the weekend. They were fishing for mackerel with impressively powerful rods. The girls doing most of the work, reeling in and re-casting, while the boys sunbathed fully clothed on a couple of recliners after lunch.

The light was amazing and I sat out most of the afternoon on a rickety chair with my head in the shade and my legs in the sun. There wasn't anything else to do. And if there was, I wasn't interested.

An old man carrying plastic bags of hand-carved spoons wandered in and I bought a couple off him. Very pale, lightweight wood. Not very durable I thought but elegant in their rustic way. But, it turned out that they were dishwasher proof and have become my wife's favourite wooden spoons for cooking.

There were some sunbeds but no beach. Instead there was a long and downright dangerous-looking jetty. I walked to the end and could see that the water was about twenty feet deep here. The sandy bottom clearly visible through the very clear water. It looked inviting but the breeze was too chilly. Down on the bottom, a single octopus was making her way along, changing colour as she encountered a rock or some weeds. No-one here was playing loud music. There was no traffic noise, nor plane in the sky or even the chug of a fishing boat. This view and its attendant quietude hadn't changed for millennia. I felt lucky to experience it.

In my cabin I switched on the TV and went for a shower. When I emerged, Michael Portillo was on the box, holding his Bradshaw's railway gazetteer and alighting from a train at Holbrook Junction on the Isle of White. The TV was black and white but I imagined his jacket was Aquascutum turquoise and his trousers Basingstoke red. I switched him off.

◆•▶

That night at the restaurant there was a lively birthday party. I was sitting alone and they invited me to join their table. I didn't get many of the side-splitting jokes, but the welcome was genuine and warm. We had plenty of beer and I donated a bottle of raki and then the dancing started.

14

THE CALL OF THE OWL

I awoke at around seven-ish with a banging headache. I couldn't remember getting back to my room. 'Oh dearie me!' The room was stuffy and hot, the sun already up and doing its thing. I threw on some clothes, delving under the bed for my socks and my head spinning when I looked up. 'Ouch! Raki…never again.' I thought and headed to the restaurant for some iced water and a coffee.

As I was putting my bag in the car a tribe of long-haired and quite large billy goats ran into the parking area and made their way towards the kitchen. The cook came out with a pan and a ladle, banging them together to scare them out of the compound.

There were plenty more about as we climbed back up the steep and unmade road. They were crowding onto the track munching thistles and several times we had to shoulder our way through them. Inquisitive noses and their strange goaty eyes peering through the open passenger door window.

We passed a strangely designed radar station that looked like the weird spiral sculpture by Anish Kapoor

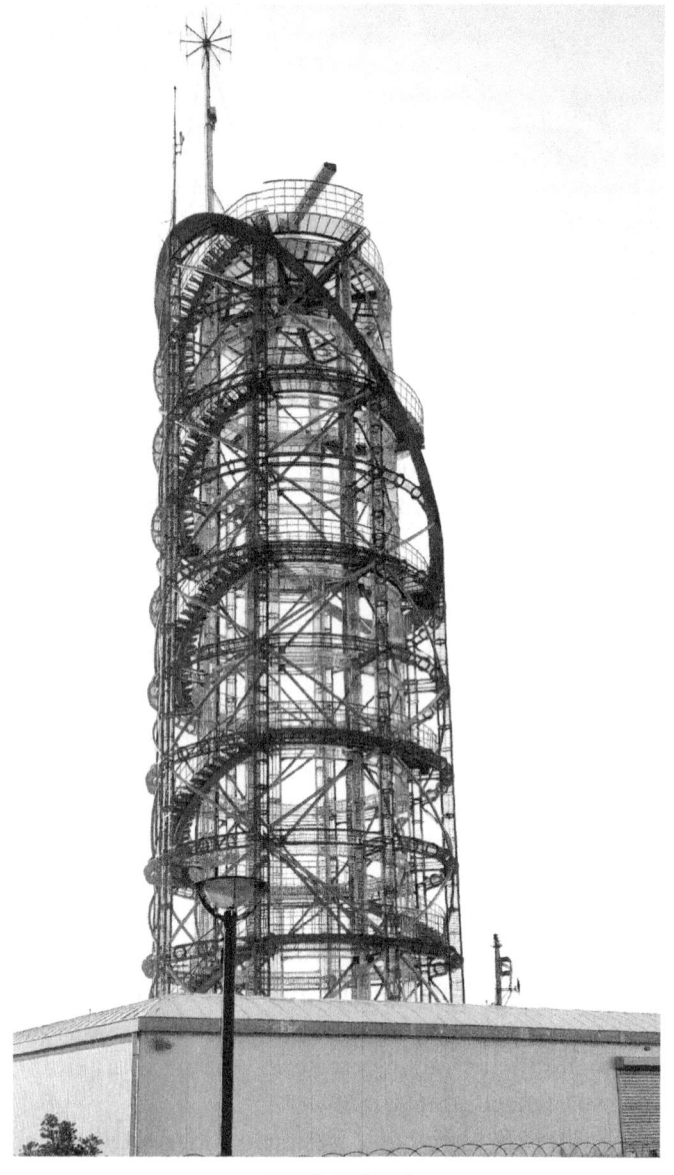

RADAR STATION

that had gone up outside the Millennium Dome.

The same hamlet appeared that we'd passed the day before. The two-storey houses in a good state of repair but gathered around that bright green and unhealthy-looking pond. I wondered what the people who lived here did for a living.

I stopped to take a picture of it and gained the attention of an old man, sitting on a large log and dressed in a dishevelled black suit and hat.

On we went. The road shining like a river of gold in the early sun. A red squirrel darted out towards the car but thought better of it. A hunter with rifle over his shoulder disappeared through a hedge.

At Assos we turned off the black top and went up and up over cobbles that set everything rattling, including my crowns. We got to the top and the road ran out at a square of sorts with cafes and restaurants. No-one was here at this hour.

In a little shop I bought a bottle of water and a helpful chap said I could park next to his restaurant so I could do the rest on foot. I went steeply upwards through narrow alleys lined with tourist tat. It was early. Just after eight.

'I am the first?' I asked the man in the ticket office.

He nodded gravely, 'You are first.'

◆•▶

The Temple of Athena is the crowning glory of the antique site of Assos. The walls are the most intact structures but even they had been raided at some point to build a castle down the coast.

A finely made path of local stone ran for a kilometre down to the agora, gymnasium and baths. There in the settlement's meeting point, were the remains of shops on three levels. The Greeks had malls thousands of years before our first shops appeared at Bath and Chester in Georgian times.

I went back up to the temple. Only a few columns were left to show the size and outline.

A whip-thin freckled snake curled ahead of me and disappeared down a crack in the rocks. Probably thinking, 'Bloody tourists and at this time in the morning? I was barely getting warmed up!'

I was still alone. A light breeze took the edge off the building heat. I sat in the shade of an oak – it had strange, holly-like leaves but was definitely an oak, with acorns – and gazed out over the glittering sea.

◆•▶

There are moments like this when you are confronted with such beauty that you can't open your eyes wide enough. No photograph could capture it. You want to drink it in. As Joe Orton said, 'An experience for the retina, and no mistake.'

I sat there looking out over the olive trees running to a small peninsula, surrounded by light with the harsh bounce of diamonds playing on the Aegean.

I thought, you will never be here again. It will never be the same, and that to me is the essence. The transitory nature of things in an always-on, immediately accessible world. It can't be bought. They can never take this away from you. Whoever they may be.

As I wandered out through the turnstiles, the soft whirr of the slush puppy machines returned me to that imperfect world. I walked back down through the alley and a party of noisy schoolkids were coming the other way.

◆•▶

When I got back to the car the restaurant had opened and had surrounded my car with chairs and tables laid with glasses. There was only – by my reckoning – just the narrowest gap to back the car out. Several men were sitting around and taking an interest but I ignored them. I got in, put the car in reverse and showed them what a few decades of on-street town parking had taught me. I knew Pedro's dimensions very well. No cutlery was dislodged, no glass was trembled as I executed a perfect three-point turn and then rolled down the hill.

◆•▶

In the afternoon, I arrived at the Hirsirlik Hotel on the outskirts of Troy. Hisirlik means 'old ruin'. An appropriate place then to lay my bones. The hotel is built to resemble some ancient temple, with columns in front of the massive dining room and bedrooms above. It's run by the Askin family – three brothers – and Mustapha Askin was to be my guide.

I started off my Troy visit with the modern and beautifully presented museum just across the road.

'Go and do that first.' said Mustapha, 'then, when

MUSTAPHA ASKIN, MY GUIDE AT TROY

we've got rid of these tour groups, we'll drive down to the site.'

A six-floored cube clad in Corten and plate glass, the museum was excellent and informative and most importantly, air conditioned. Each floor is linked by a ramp and takes you up – floor by floor – closer to the present day.

There were some lovely pieces of delicate jewellery, but Schliemann's selling-off to Athens of the big treasure still rankled.

Schliemann was a German businessman who had made a fortune during the Crimean War. He was also an amateur archaeologist and dedicated himself to the excavation of Troy. Among the many controversies surrounding him was his discovery of several important artefacts and fabulous items of jewellery at the site, which he subsequently sold off to the Greeks. A source of great bitterness among the Turks. Understandably.

The stories about that treasure and where it had wound up with Turkish secret agents hot on the heels of Schliemann, are worthy of a Dan Brown thriller.

Back across the road at the hotel, the Askin brothers were inundated with bus-loads of Spanish tourists. I sat out on the roadside and watched as they dispatched over two hundred covers in the space of an hour and a half. It was so busy that I went and got my own beers from the fridge and wrote them down.

Then, just as I was dropping off, Mustapha eating okra off a plate with a fork, shouts to me. 'Okay, let's go!'

Trained as an engineer, he's been guiding at the Troy archaeological site for 45 years. He made sense of the place that I would never have understood – despite my interest – merely by walking around. I watched other tourists scratch their heads as they looked at the tumbled walls and tried to decipher the panels of visitor information. I won't bore you, dear reader, with our conversations, but Mustapha was informative and gently revealing, dispelling many questions I have had over the years.

He agreed with me that most archaeologists were too scientific and would not embrace the myth and the story that was so central to most people. That story had started with the Judgement of Paris and the abduction of a Greek queen, resulting in the launching of a thousand ships. The whole romance of the place was lost to them. So, I was somewhat pleased that he hadn't heard of my travelling companion (the book by John Gaskin) and was unaware of Gaskin's recommendation to secure the services of Mustapha as a guide. 'If he can be found.'

I couldn't let my copy go but I promised to send him one.

We stood where Hector – to my mind, the real hero of the Iliad – had fallen. We looked out at the burial mounds across the Hellespont where the big Greek names lay still. We discussed the importance of the site to the Romans and how Virgil had made it their own story by writing The Aeneid.

I took his photograph and he asked if he looked okay? I said he looked very handsome but perhaps it was time to change the photograph on his official guide badge?

‹•›

The truth is that no-one really knows the truth. About the connection between the myth and the physical site, no-one can honestly say. But, the site exists and its important location for trade between east and west is obvious, both overland and by sea. The square-sailed ships couldn't enter the Dardanelles unless the wind was right and were sometimes delayed for weeks here trying to get to Constantinople. The caravanserai all stopped here to meet them from their treks from the east.

And the book exists, too – The Iliad, with its 16,000 lines of prose. Anyone who has read it feels the pull to believe and be part of the story. To come here is to make a pilgrimage of sorts and as with any experience, be it religious or secular, it pays to have a good guide.

15

HAMMAM AND HAIRCUT

I awoke in the King Priam room of the Hisirlik Hotel. I wondered if the poor man had had better digs than these at Troy. He was however long gone, his problems over.

I struggled in the telephone box-sized bathroom. The shower wouldn't work above knee height and barely dribbled below that. I got my stretching done early just trying to get the soap off.

Wet rooms? Hmmm, not sure. Fine if you have palatial space, I suppose, but when you have to remove the mat, towels and toilet roll before you start, not so good.

I hadn't slept all that well. The guard dogs were barking and chasing around at intervals. When they weren't barking they were keening for something and just as I dropped off they'd start up again.

I sat on the bed and examined my toe with a Simon Templar eyebrow. It looked more like the one on the opposite foot now. For which I was belatedly grateful. I had hardly noticed it scrambling over the ruins yesterday. How typical that when something hurts your day is blighted, but when nothing hurts, we take it for granted. Note to self to be more mindful, in a truly Epicurean manner.

Downstairs I was treated to a thin omelette and salad with some excellent coffee.

Out on the road there were fields of tomatoes with gangs of women bent double picking them. They were wearing the usual garb of headscarves and baggy trousers. A couple had small babies on their backs and I could see a few of them eating as they went.

Then a man selling cucumbers. They were in a heap almost as high as he was. Dumped from a tractor onto the side of the dual carriageway. A hard day's selling lay ahead for him.

We parked up at an Otopark in the big town of Cannakale.

Otopark is the Turkish word for car park or auto-park. Many English expressions and words have been adopted over the years and spelled phonetically. The Turkish word for taxi is taksi. Otoparks are very safe and guarded places to leave your car and usually centrally convenient.

Cannakale sits on the sea facing the Gallipoli Peninsula. It was to here that Leander swam across the strait every night to visit his beloved Hero, priestess to Aphrodite. Guided every night by the lantern in her tower. Until the wind blew it out one evening and the poor bloke drowned.

Also drowned was the princess Helles who had helped Jason retrieve the Golden Fleece. Which was how the mouth of the straits had got its name, Hellespont. There are references to her all over the town.

A TYPICAL STREET IN CANNAKALE

I had found an apartment – that had been listed as a hotel – where I could get some washing done and stop moving for a bit.

The very friendly owner was expansive about the problems he was facing with the economy at its worst ever. I pointed to the washing powder in bags running up the staircase behind him.

He said, 'I found this lot at last month's prices so I bought 100 kilos. The price of everything is going crazy.'

I congratulated him on cornering the Persil market.

We had a deep and meaningful over a delicious Turkish coffee that he rustled up at the desk. We both agreed that everything was going to shit when it really need not. He described with barely concealed disgust the incompetence of the government. Meanwhile, above our heads a six-metre-high banner with a picture of President Erdogan wafted between the buildings.

I walked out into the street towards the nearest hammam but it was closed. So, I retraced my steps to find the other one at the opposite end of town.

I almost missed it. A hole in the wall where I was greeted and shown to a cabin to disrobe. The whole place was laid in marble and slippery under the sliders – no socks – I'd been given to wear. I followed the masseur like an old man who'd had his roller skates confiscated.

He led me to a sauna room that was so hot I couldn't place my feet on the floor. After 20 minutes I was beckoned to a slightly cooler chamber, where my masseur put on a glove made of Scotch Brite and scoured my body all over. Then a dousing with tepid water and more scrubbing. Then to the heated marble altar. Before I got on, I pointed to the 3-4 lumbar joint where I'd had two operations on my lower back and acted out the charade of breaking a breadstick. He nodded, soaped me up and got going.

Crikey! He had hands like Maximus Prime! My body complained by parts. 'Ooooh, helloooo!' said my calves. 'Give it a rest!' clicked my shoulder blades. 'Oh my God!' said my kneecaps, as they settled back down from my hips.

Then it was over and the dousing and rubbing continued in a cool room. Followed by a shower so powerful it had me bent over.

He manhandled me into a chair and rubbed me dry. Covered my head and body with dry towels and left me in companionable silence with three other blokes sporting soup-strainer moustaches.

Tea was served and all was right with the world. If ever there was a Marlboro Light moment, this was it. The whole process a little over an hour and a half and for a fee of £3.50.

Emerging into the sunlight I felt like a newly scraped Jersey potato, marvellously calm and my whole body shining with energy.

I went back to get a small bag from Pedro and found the guard washing a car in the lot next door. He gestured that the key was on top of the front tyre. And that's where I found it. And that's where I replaced it. When in Rome, eh?

My building was in a street lined with barbers, so I had a trim. Again, a very discreet, soothing and relaxing service, where care was taken without rush. But it was a little freaky to see most of the customers sitting around wearing face packs in every colour you could imagine. It was like a scene from Spirited Away.

❦

Feeling restored – and with my washing drying on a rack in the apartment – I walked out into the glowing evening light for a stroll along the front.

I felt I knew this place and had seen it in a film, *The Wild Pear Tree*, by Turkish director Nuri Bilge Ceylan. It was very much a modern city and mostly made up of low-rise concrete buildings. Very little of the old architectural features remained.

There was a museum and docked next to it the mine-layer that had caused so much damage to our fleet in 1914. Three of our capital ships sunk and a further three badly damaged. Not one of Churchill's (then First Lord of the Admiralty) better days.

Walking along this generous waterfront I came to a square with yet another wooden horse. Asking a passer-by, I was told that this was the one that had been in the film Troy and had been donated to the city as a thank you. I'd refused to photograph the version at the entrance to Troy itself. A truly monstrous and boxy thing that looked like it was made of scaffold boards.

Although the 'Trojan Horse' is perhaps the most famous myth associated with the Trojan War, it is – to my mind – also the saddest part of that legend. A proud city succumbing to a dirty trick after ten years of siege. It doesn't get a mention in The Iliad and only briefly makes an appearance in The Odyssey.

A little further along there were seven identical stands selling toasted cobs of sweet corn. Begging an obvious question. I looked but I couldn't tell them apart.

Still in the afterglow of my bath experience I watched the sun set on the Dardanelles over a couple of bottles of Efes, the local beer, and retired without supper.

16

TOUR OF DUTY

Dur yolcu! Bilmeden gelip bastığın,
Bu toprak, bir devrin battığı yerdir.

Those words are written in large letters on the cliff-face across the water on the Gallipoli Peninsular side of the strait. So large are the letters that you can read them from Cannakale on the opposite side where I was staying. Here, the pinch point of the Dardanelles, less than two kilometres across, has been guarded for centuries by a brace of matched forts, one either side.

I'd asked my landlord about those words and he'd read me the translation. It's part of a poignant poem about the tragedy of war. The first stanza reads:

Stop traveller!
On this ground you tread on, an epic lies.
Bow down, lend your ear, for this silent hill
Is where the heart of a nation sighs.

BEACH WHERE THE FIRST ALLIES LANDED, GALLIPOLI PENINSULAR

Whether or not you are interested in the campaign that was fought here (by mainly Australian and New Zealand troops), what happened in the nine months of trench warfare was the very birth of a nation. It was to lead the fading Ottoman empire into the nation state of Turkey.

A brilliant Turkish commander, battle-hardened by campaigns in the Balkans and elsewhere, was to change the course of the First World War. If the allies had won here it might have been over by the end of 1915. Maybe. But, they would have captured Istanbul and opened supply lines to Russia to create a properly forceful second front against the Germans.

However, that was not to be. High-handedness by the British brought the Ottomans out of their neutrality against the allies. With tragic consequences.

Ironically, the Allies' only successful operation of the campaign came at the very end with the eventual withdrawal and evacuation of nearly 90,000 troops without a single loss. But among them were thousands of wounded and men suffering from frostbite. In total 97 thousand dead on both sides by the end of the campaign.

The allied survivors – who had already endured months of awful privations with a weak supply line – were then sent to fight in the nightmare of the Western Front in France and Belgium. A very long road home for them.

Mustapha Kemal was a brilliant Turkish commander. He pushed his troops and led from the front. When he was hit by shrapnel he was saved by his pocket watch. He was destined to become a national hero, to become Mustapha Kemal Atatürk and to lead the republic of Turkey. A most brilliant and modern man. He overhauled the country and brought it together in an almost Solomonic way.

Our Turkish guide, Bulent, had been doing these battlefield tours for twenty years. He spoke English with a 'strine' accent. But he said he could also do a decent 'Nah Zeelund'. He had been an advisor on the film *Gallipoli* and took us to the very places featured in the movie. But after the tour I found that I couldn't rewatch the film. It had depressed me enough the first time round.

He told us that Australian troops were nick-named 'diggers' due to the number of earthworks they were forced to excavate. That the opposing trenches were sometimes only 15 yards apart. That the youngest to die was James Martin, only 14.

But the graveyards said it all really. They were sad but beautifully maintained. The wind sighing through the pines.

The whole bottom half of the peninsula is covered in trees now and kept as a memorial. Nobody can build here. But at the time there was no cover, all timber having been logged for firewood against the hard winters. Coming ashore in the amphibious landings was deadly. I took a photograph of the first beach to take casualties. The continuous lapping of the waves had caused a gun emplacement to come adrift from the shoreline and now leant at an angle, its rusty door frozen open.

At the Lone Pine cemetery, which marks a famous battle, the eponymous pine had been reduced to a stump by shellfire.

ANZAC troops had taken home pine cones as souvenirs and in 1990 a seedling from a cone from the original pine – grown by an Australian relative – was returned to the site to be planted as a replacement. Bulent, the guide, had remembered the planting ceremony and looked upon it almost like a brother.

'We have grown up together, and got wider at the waist,' he said.

The memorial here is understated and the cross carved in relief into the cenotaph-shaped stonework so that it did not project and offend the Turks.

◆•▶

Then we moved on to the Turkish memorial with its strange pi-shaped monument and communal graves.

I stood chatting with Bulent and we fed crisps to some large stray dogs. 'These dogs come from nowhere,' he said. 'They know the tourists will feed them. They've all been sterilised but they just seem to keep coming.' With a shrug he got everyone back on the bus to return to the ferry. Everyone was quiet on the ride back and filled with individual thoughts about what we'd seen. It had been an affecting day and a lesson to reject hubris if you can see it in yourself.

◆•▶

After it was all over, Atatürk returned. He made a poignant speech that showed his statesmanship.

'You, the mothers who sent their sons from far away countries, wipe away your tears. Your sons are now lying in our bosom and are in peace. After having lost their lives on this land they have become our sons as well.'

17

TURKEY LEFTOVERS

On the ferry back to Cannakale I'd met Brenda from Melbourne and Simone from Limerick. Both travelling alone and both great fun.

Brenda – who seemed to have no safety valve when it came to being candid – said that she was really enjoying the attentions of the men here. Within four hours of landing at Istanbul she'd been wined, dined and laid. That wasn't happening for her at home, where she'd been through what she described as 'a decade-long dry patch.'

Simone was relatively modest by comparison and had been travelling for months in Siberia and Mongolia before moving on to China. Now she was slowly wending her way home. She had a whacking great camera that she continuously snapped away with on motor-drive, taking three photos of everything she looked at.

The ferry had run out of beer so I repaired to my favourite bar on the waterfront. The waiter recognised me from the previous day and guided me to a table inside out of the wind, where he had my ice-cold Efes waiting. He was eating pide, a kind of Turkish pizza, and offered to share it with me.

TURKEY LEFTOVERS

AN OK GAME

On the table next to me, four girls in their late teens were playing a riotous tile game that looked like a cross between Scrabble and Mah-Jong. I asked what the game was called.

'Okey!' they said in unison.

'Okay?' I said.

'Okey' they all nodded.

'Okay!' I said and returned to my table amid squeals of laughter.

◆•▶

Next morning, while it was still dark, I sat on the edge of the bed for the daily toe inspection. The offending tarsal was still a funny shape. All toes are I suppose, but I was comparing it to its brothers. However, I now had two bad toes. The little piggy on the left was coloured like Joseph's famous coat. 'Ah – aaah – aaaah,' I sang to myself. This one I'd stubbed in the dark the night before in the bathroom on a jutting tile around the shower. The tiler had just left it sticking out instead of cutting it. Okay, never mind, I still had eight good ones left.

The skin was now scabbing over nicely where I'd badly grazed my knuckles in Chios. Pulling the door shut behind me without looking, my hand had encountered a razor-sharp strip of draught excluder. I didn't make that mistake again.

Then my elbow where I'd banged it in Loutakia had settled to a yellowish purple bruise. That too seemed to be on the mend.

All this must, I realise, make me seem like a right Captain Clumsy. But in my defence, you can't out-think the local builders here. In my shower there were bare wires taped up. I didn't know if they were live, but I considered them out of range of the shower head. Plug sockets were falling out of walls. I could go on. A healthy sense of self-preservation was being paid for with a few scrapes.

At my digs, the owner, Mustapha, beckoned me over for a welcome coffee and we sat down under President Erdogan's stern gaze for a chat. I said that I had thought about returning via Iznik but had decided against.

'Ahah, my father lives in Iznik!'

He went on to relate that – apart from its coloured tiles and ceramics – Iznik was famed for its buried treasure. That – during some purge – the residents had thrown their gold down wells in the town rather than carry it with them. Recently several big finds had been made.

'My father has a well in his garden,' he said.

His father hadn't been interested in treasure-hunting and so he'd covered it over with a lawn but now and again people would show up and say, 'We think you have a well here.' Which he always denied.

Eventually Mustapha convinced him to investigate. They dug a hole in the lawn and uncapped the well. Mustapha went down 15 metres until he hit dirt. Then over the course of several summers dug down a further six metres.

'It was tough work, the well was narrow and I am tall. And you can't really send a kid down there.'

I thought about that Dickensian idea and chuckled inwardly.

But they found nothing. His father said, 'I told you so,' and shook his head laughing. 'Perhaps if I had dug another six metres?' said Mustapha wistfully.

◆•▶

I found Pedro at the Otopark. He looked like he had a bit of a flat tyre on the front driver's side. I kicked it to see, which set my toe grumbling and made me smile at my idiocy.

On the motorway it was sunny and hung with a Remington sky. I passed substantial roadside fruit stands right on the eight-lane highway. There was very little traffic and respect for motorway rules were few. A couple of big BMWs hacked past doing over 120 mph by my estimate. A police car was on the opposite carriageway but facing the same way as us.

The glittering blue of the Dardanelles was off to port. The giant suspension bridge a smudge of a line in the far distance. On the right-hand side the country looked like wheat to me. Rolling hills of harvested fields bestrode by electricity pylons.

I was bored by these ridiculous roads now. Nobody was on them. Sometimes, for periods of ten minutes or so, I was the only traffic in any direction. I thought how much fun it would be on this perfect surface to blat along in a fast car at 200 mph.

But more to the point, I resented this motorway heaven. Every time we'd tried to by-pass them and explore locally we'd find the road would run out or be redirected back. Which was why I suppose you had tractors and old men on stink-wheels going in the opposite direction and down the hard shoulder. It was the only way they could get to work.

I recalled how my historian friend Caroline Finkel had bemoaned the loss of so many ancient roads, some of them pre-dating the Romans by centuries. The Turks would appropriate them and tarmac over the old stones or run walls or bridges through them, making for long workarounds for foot travellers. I wasn't sure why I felt so annoyed by this when we have done the same to the Roman roads of Britain.

◆•▶

Now, on the left, a massive black and white cinder block of a ship appeared, barely shaped at the front. It was getting along quite well. As we crossed the mega suspension bridge to the European side, the brick appeared under us and now on the right.

Soon the top of the Aegean appeared, and in the clear air I could see the curve that marked its limit and the promise of Greece.

I stopped at a dusty petrol station and topped up the tank to get rid of some of my Turkish. When I went in to pay, the kid in the shop tried to sell me twenty-five kilos of rice on special offer.

'Is a very good price sir!'

◆•▶

For a while we'd been starting to see big Turkish flags. I knew this meant we were close to the border. And then we reached it, a typically massive affair in the late

Ottoman Asda supermarket style. All for show and very expensive. Hugely tall concrete pillars held up curved structures high above, from which some of the cladding was already missing. I hoped no more would drop while we waited in the queue.

I fed a stray dog pretzels out the window. He disappeared and then appeared on the passenger side. He wanted some of my emergency wine gums but I wound up the window. He then made a good job of licking off the bird dirt.

We then proceeded along four windows where my passport was presented each time. I had to get out to hand it over so I pushed the car forwards between windows.

At the third the guard said, 'Your car is broken?'

'No,' I replied.

At the last window the guard asked 'What is your name?' He was staring at me and holding my passport. I told him. He shrugged and said, 'You go!'

Then there was another hold up with two armed squaddies. Index fingers straight above the trigger guards of their M4s. They looked bored. Perhaps this was not what they had signed up for. But they'd been signed up for it all the same. Eventually a barely perceptible nod and we drove over the terribly maintained bridge. It was domed with anthill-sized tarmac and there were holes, too, where you could see the channel choked with rushes below. It was in such a state. I guessed that no-one knew which side owned it.

Then a booth with a smiling girl. 'Welcome to Greece, sir!'

We bowled down the Via Egnatia – the old Roman route from Rome to Byzantium. Fine views of the coastline. We passed Kavala, from where I had visited the ancient site of Phillipi years before.

Then traffic was stopped while a military column of tanks on low-loaders crossed our lane from a side road. They were going the other way. Towards the border.

18
ISLAND LIFE

At the port the lovely lady at the ticket office had said, 'Let me reassure you, sir. You cannot miss the ferry. It is very big and orange.'

I had a couple of hours so I parked up and walked to a fancy-looking yacht club for a beer.

◆•◆

Later, and in the early afternoon, we were about 20 miles out of Alexandroupoli and slowly overhauling a fishing boat that was crossing our heading. Light blue and white and trawler-sized, with car-tyre fenders along the gunwale and an elegant prow. We passed her astern and she continued her run towards Thassos.

Inexorably the island got larger as we approached. Only 17 kilometres long and mountainous. Samothraki or Samothrace. It was from here that the god Poseidon had looked down at the mortals fighting the Trojan War. I tried to remember what Mustapha Askin had said about the significance of that. But I knew Poseidon was on the side of the Greeks, 'the people of the sea'. At least he was until the fall of Troy. The winning side had not made sufficient offerings to the gods for their success, turning both Poseidon and Athena against them. Which made for a rough passage home for the likes of Odysseus.

I stood at the back of the ferry on the top deck, buffeted by a strong breeze. The Greek flag was flying straight out like a board and was framed by the gloriously blue sea and our white wake.

In my pocket the phone vibrated, an email had flooded in. I hadn't had many. My clients had either respected my out-of-office message or had abandoned me altogether. It was from the allotments association warning of an invasion of badgers. I imagined my shed listing low at the back of my plot, slowly sinking into a badger's sett.

I then got chatting to a Greek guy and his girlfriend. He was wearing a type of headdress or scarf around his dreadlocks and was wittering on about what a mystical place the island was. Although he was pointing at Thassos and not Samothraki where the ferry was headed. I had heard that Samothraki attracted an alternative crowd and had done so since the sixties. The pair were amenable and friendly but hadn't heard of Lifebuoy and had a whiff of meat feast pizza about them. I moved to windward, saying the sun was in my eyes.

◆•▶

Approaching the harbour, we were sent down to the car deck, where they'd opened the door to the engine room.

Incredible heat was pumping out like the sauna I'd experienced the other day. I stood to one side and looked out through the wide-open cargo doors. The land was very close and moving at a sickening speed as we came up to the hard. It was like a panning shot in the cinema when you're too close to the screen. A very strange feeling when you are in a massive three-storey volume but the real world is fleeting by outside. Worlds colliding with precision. I imagined it must be close to experiencing space travel.

The ship turned in its own length within the harbour walls and reversed up to the dock. I drove Pedders across the street from the ferry and tied him off at a bar where I had a cooling ale. Then checked in to the only place to stay. A rough-looking hotel just up the road. I had to convince the lady owner to rent me a room. She told me they were closed but I persisted. After a bit of cajolery she agreed and showed me a cramped little room looking out onto a back street. She wanted 50 euros a night and I said I'd pay that, but for three nights. I didn't really want to stay that long but the ferry was already running its reduced winter service. Finally, we settled for 18 euros a night and I went looking for some supper.

◆•▶

Next day, on the bathroom's chequerboard tiling, the gecko had moved from King's Rook Three to Queen's Bishop Five. Was that even a legal move? I had never actually seen this tiny apricot-coloured chap budge. Perhaps he just thought himself from square to square?

It had been blowing a hoolie all night and I'd slept with the doors open, knowing that I was safe from the 633 Squadron.

Outside, a bright sunny day. But, for such an idyllic island, there was a heck of a racket going on. I looked out into the street. Across and at the same height, two men were stripping a roof and throwing the rubbish crashing and clanging into a truck below. They narrowly missed a man using a leaf blower but he didn't notice because he was wearing ear defenders against the dreadful noise he was making. Up the road another man mounted his two stroke and revved it to the maximum, sending a big cloud of sooty smoke into the open doorway of a house where a woman was hanging her washing. Hmmm… I had heard this was a sleepy little port. Give me sanctuary!

◆•▶

Six clicks up the road I found it. The Sanctuary of the Great Gods.

Nice segue huh?

'This is one of Greece's most mysterious archaeological sites,' said the guidebook. A temple complex, built by the Thracians around 1000 BCE. Secret rites and initiations had been held here up until the 4th century. The Temple with its secrets had been a magnet to famous characters of the ancient world. Philip II had met his bride here and their union had created Alexander the Great. Jason and his Argonauts and Odysseus are said to have visited as too had the historian Herodotus.

A fine museum, designed tastefully by a certain Stuart M Shaw of NYC, a plaque read. And a statue of winged Nike in brilliantly white marble. An exact copy of the original, which had been 3D scanned and cut from a single block. The French archaeologist who found the original had carted it off to Paris where it has since resided, gathering dust in the Louvre. But the French had generously allowed the Greeks to scan it to make their own copy. Not for the first time did I ponder the rights of foreign museums to hold onto such plunder. I'd read that there were Moroccan artefacts in the British Museum that were so sacred that not even the curators were allowed to examine them. And then were the Benin Bronzes and the Parthenon Marbles, a tricky situation to navigate.

I walked round the site trying to make out how it might have looked. Which wasn't obvious or easy. Hardly any reconstruction had been made and the blocks lay around in ranks like tombstones. There was also a lot of doubling back and retracing of steps because the modern bridges – that had been placed over the torrent that ran through the site – had been washed out. Hah, that's modern builders for you! But still, it was all lovely in the early morning light.

I tried to ask questions of the attendant but she was still in full covid garb with gloves and mask and standing so far away that we had to shout to each other.

◂•▸

I drove up and through Hora to the highest point possible by car. I was taking it easy because the road was very rough. But, I must have missed a jutting rock because something went bang underneath.

'Ouch!' cried Pedro.

When I got to the top, I laid among the grit and pebbles under the car to take a look. The bracket coupling the exhaust was pushed to one side. I wiggled a stick at it. It seemed to be holding.

Then suddenly, a terrible roaring noise – that sounded like a rockfall – had me out from under the car in a panic. Banging my head on the towing bracket in the process. Looking up, I saw with some relief that it was four fighter jets, buzzing the mountain. But I couldn't make out any markings on them as to whether they were Greek or Turkish.

◆•▶

Down the road on the other side of Fengari, the peak that Poseidon had sat upon, we came to a couple of restaurants that are famous for roast goat. But both were shut for the winter.

We drove onwards and downhill, and eventually to a fine sandy beach on the other side of the island. I was the only person there. Quite a spot, the sea glittering in dazzling diamonds that made you squint despite wearing sunglasses against the glare.

I parked Pedders up where the beach sand was still packed firmly and walked over to meet Nicolas, the bar owner. A wiry old goat of a man with a wild beard and sun-blackened skin. It was his last day of the season.

'You are in luck my friend. The beers are on me.' And together we began to clear his fridges of Mythos lager.

BAR OWNER - NICOLAS

He said that every day in August he had over two thousand paying customers. It had been his busiest year and he had been packing up. I rested my beer on a giant speaker – thankfully quiet now – and he brought across some spicy flatbreads and sausages, all on the house.

I asked what he did in the winter.

'I like Scotland,' he said.

'Not too cold for you?' I asked.

'No, nothing compared to here. Thick snow on the beach every wintertime. The only way I can get here is by boat during the cold months.'

I gazed out at the glittering sea and shimmering heat haze from the shade of the bar's awning. It was hard to imagine.

He'd put up welcoming flags of every nation, and I told him that he had the Union Flag upside down. He was fascinated when I drew how it should be and said he'd change that next year.

'In all these years, you are the only Englishman to tell me that.'

By and by, a couple of German women came over.

'Lesbians.' he muttered.

I asked how he knew.

'Oh they're lesbians alright. These German girls all are. Believe me I've tried!'

They asked if they could rent a boat. 'Thirty euro,' he told them. They didn't like that.

'What if only one of us takes the boat and the other one walks around the bay. She gets seasick, you see?'

'Still 30 euro.' Said Nicolas with a shrug. 'Wanna drink?'

They shook their heads.

'Have you got a toilet?' One of them asked.
'No, sorry. You want pissy? Go behind rocks!'
They sauntered off.

Then a Romanian dentist from Bucharest joined the party. He walked towards us like a mirage in a black armless top and dazzling black and white board shorts.

His name was Vlad. I immediately thought of Vlad the Impaler. What a name for a dentist. He said he was taking a break from work. He felt burnt out. He was also very worried about the war in Ukraine. The Black Sea only two hours drive from where he lived.

He turned out to be an entertaining person and here we three sat for the rest of the afternoon. Drifting in and out of conversation and trying to cope with overpowering perfection of it all.

◆•▶

The next day. Up early and out on the road to Kipos Beach. Where the road finally runs out as it hits a mountain. There was nobody there and nothing doing. Everything definitely over at this spot. There was not a tree in sight. The surrounding cliffs forming a bowl of scree around a turning circle. It was an inhospitable place. The foreshore strewn with jagged boulders running down to a beach of grey shale. I picked my way through it, taking care not to rick an ankle.

The coast road was clinging on by its fingernails. Landslips had taken out small sections and the crash barrier hung limply in many places, completely suspended in clear air.

There were small rockfalls from the brown bluffs that

edged the land side of the road. Around a corner I hit a wayward boulder that clattered under the car. Luckily it was made of shale and shattered. Scattering across the carriageway in the rearview mirror. Pedro raised a quizzical eyebrow at the nut behind the steering wheel.

All along this stretch, where the road was close to sea level, were fords where small rivers ran down to the sea. They were filled with basketball-sized rocks that were hard work to drive over, the interior of the car swaying at mad angles. Not something to splash through. I thought what a nightmare this road would be at night.

The torrents that come off the mountain are famed for their brutal nature in spring. On the way back we crossed the most famous of them at Fournios Gorge. The river here is known as 'The Murderer' for its flash floods, taking out the odd, unsuspecting hiker every other year. A small coachload of American tourists was

THE MILDLY ALARMING ROAD TO KIPOS BEACH

gathered around in floppy hats and plaid shirts, taking snaps.

Then on to lovely cool glades of oaks and ferns growing among the car-sized boulders. Very pretty. People were camping here and skinny dipping at the water's edge.

We stopped off at a village famed for its hot springs and waterfalls an hour and a half's trek up the mountain. In the empty square a shirtless, lean and muscled man was chopping logs and I envied his pecs and lats. He had the physique of a rock climber.

I wasn't up for a hike with my clutch foot in such poor condition, sadly. My friend Caroline Finkel, an expert on Ottoman history, had raved about it. She'd been talking about the 1970s but the place was still full of young hippies who were wild camping in the woods next to the falls. There was quite a bit of nudity going on as they sauntered out between the sunbeams among the boulders, pine trees and lush ferns. Some were washing dishes at the water's edge, others reading well-thumbed paperbacks. It all looked idyllic.

A quick coffee in the lovely village also known as Samothraki and then back to the port. Where a freighter, the Mikaelis K, was offloading ammunition. Army trucks were carting it off with a police and fire brigade escort.

I had my first souvlaki. Cooked pink and delicious. I thought of my mother warning against undercooked pork. She would be shaking her head at such risk-taking.

◆•▶

That night, low in the sky, a most strange crescent moon. Blood red and very clear. Appropriately hanging over the Turkish coast. I thought I'd try a kebab from the van on the hard.

Inside this static caravan affair was a very large woman. The van creaked as she moved with the dainty precision of Oliver Hardy, her hips narrowly avoiding the charcoal grill on one side and the boiling chip pan on the other. I made the gesture that said 'give me the works' and she got started.

Behind me was a man in a hurry so I stood aside. He shouted his order and ran the few yards to the harbour wall where the navigation lights of a small motor cruiser were approaching fast out of the gloom.

The man spoke into a walkie-talkie, and I realised that he must be the harbour master. The cruiser damn near rammed the wall and he had a hard time shoving her off. A lot of shouting went on. On the boat were three men who had been fishing for the day. All were a bit giggly.

They half-heartedly threw ropes to the man on the quay, but they fell short and kept dropping into the water. Finally, he got the bow line around a bollard and handed it back to the guy on the front, turning to the man on the stern. I noticed that the bow line had again been let slip from lifeless fingers into the water. It then occurred to both me and to him that the three men in the boat were completely paralytic.

Exasperated, he turned to see me watching, and I offered to help. He shook his head and gestured at me not to move. At this point both ropes were thrown simultaneously at him, hitting his turned back. Causing

KEBAB VAN, SAMOTHRAKI PORT

much laughter from the cabin cruiser. He stooped to pick them up. Coiled them neatly and hurled them back aboard. Picked up his kebab and walked off into the darkness.

Now the men aboard the cruiser were adrift in the harbour with a stalled engine. I sat on a plastic chair and watched them try to restart it, while picking at my kebab. Shouts and falling over and general frustrated swearing. Finally, they drifted alongside a freighter where a nightwatchman threw them a line.

The kebab was a complete meal and had the strongest onions I'd ever eaten, making my eyes water.

◀•▶

In my pension I was still the only guest.

After three nights I'd got used to being locked in alone and sat in the empty saloon reading. At 10pm there was a power cut, so I climbed the stairs to my room, fumbling along in the pitch dark.

ISLAND LIFE

Sound asleep and at 3am, everything came on again. Lights, AC, even the TV at full volume, which I didn't think I'd ever turned on. Fully awake now, the power immediately went out again. I spent some time with the torch making sure everything was off.

◆•▶

Next morning, there was still no electricity, so I paid the elderly owner in cash. She then opened up her reservations book and asked how did the first week of May 2023 suit me? She could give me two weeks. 'Special price!' I said I'd think about it.

Then there followed an exchange where she insisted we pal up on Facebook. I told her I wasn't on Facebook any longer. But she made me show her every screen of my phone's apps to prove it.

I was hoping for breakfast in my favourite taverna. The chef was making coffee on a camping stove and defrosting chicken quarters with a blow torch. Could she make me some eggs, I asked.

'No, only coffee. No light,' she said, pointing to a plug socket.

I thought of how many times I'd cooked up a full English on a primus stove in the woods. But then I'd been a boy scout.

We met up with Vlad the dentist and his red Cherokee on the dock and travelled back to Alexandroupoli together.

He was driving the eight hours back to Bucharest that evening. He asked me what my direction was after Greece. I said that I was tempted by Sicily, Sardinia and

Corsica, and from there up through France. He looked at me sternly.

'Nic, you must go back through the Balkans. They are so beautiful. And the way it's going there politically, it might be your last chance for a few years.'

The voice of a central European who was more in tune than me. Hmmm, I thought, maybe he's right.

◆•◆

Alexandroupoli, named after the Great Alex. What to say about it? It has a lighthouse.

To be honest, I was a bit fagged out and it was hot and humid compared to the wild and windy island I'd just left. I tried to change some money, but Western Union had – only minutes before – shut for the weekend.

Late afternoon I found a backstreet restaurant with locals fairly comforted after a long Saturday lunch. The patron recommended the mussel salad.

'Last of the year,' he said.

THE FRIENDLY STAFF OF THE POUMBIS RESTAURANT IN ALEXANDROUPOLI

They were stupendous. I thought I must do them for Dad like this. Olive oil, lemon and parsley. So simple. So good.

There were several tables of young people. All very civilised. At home they'd all be in Pizza Express, keeping out of the rain.

Then baby red snapper in a light batter. Very fresh. I put my hands together in a prayer of gratitude to the owner, chef and waitress. Hope is alive and well and thriving at the Poumbis Restaurant.

So then, what to say about Alexandroupoli apart from its lighthouse? A nice port town with a good welcome and treasure to be found for those that have eyes to see.

19

KASSANDRA CROSSING

Out of Thrace and into Macedonia.

A chilly morning with dew on Pedds, parked in a side street. The curling lacquer on the roof was coming off nicely, but unfortunately now starting on the bonnet. How long before the car was completely stripped of this stuff. Hard to know.

I spotted the ice scraper in a side pocket and thought I'd help the process along. A man walking along with a bag of bread stopped to watch this mad Englishman apparently de-icing his roof. I smiled at him, and he walked on without expression.

In the hotel pension the desk manager had offered me a coffee. While he was in the back making it, I helped myself from a large jar of boiled sweets for my onward journey. Stuffing them in my back pocket before he caught me at it. But now I had to sit on one cheek for comfort. He had a bad back and when I sympathised he then relayed his back's life history. After 20 minutes another arrival allowed me to slip discreetly into the street.

Starting off I noticed some clutch judder. Oh-oh!

But after the hammering I'd given Pedro for 80,000 miles I only had myself to blame. I was sure it'd be fine once he warmed up.

We passed Kavala on the coast and then the ancient site of Philippi. Named for Philip of Macedonia.

I'd been around it on a blisteringly hot day in August when we'd had a couple a couple of weeks on the island of Thassos. I'd taken myself off on the 7am ferry to Kavala. The bus on the other side had to toot its horn at the bus stops to wake up sleepy shop girls going into work. I'd almost got heatstroke walking over the vast site, seeing where St Paul had been imprisoned and reliving the days when Mark Anthony had defeated Cassius and Brutus in huge land battles. The result was the end of the Roman Republic, Octavian became the first Emperor and the beginning of two centuries of Pax Romana.

◆•▶

VLAD

On the road it was massively windy. The car rocked and the roof bars howled. But I loved driving with the windows down, so pulled a light jacket from the back seat and put it on while holding the wheel with my knees.

Then up into the mountains. A sign read, 'University of Forest Taxidermists'. Really?

I stopped at the top to fill up. A tiny petrol stand. Just two old-fashioned pumps with sight glasses, straight out of an Edward Hopper painting. The owner sitting out of the wind on a cane chair. I asked him if it was always so windy?

'Yesterday there was nothing and it was 35 degrees,' he shrugged.

After some fine views we went downhill to the left-hand finger of the Halkadiki Peninsula. The one called Kassandra. The neck of this digit is so narrow I could almost touch the sea out of both car windows.

We reached Loutra, where I was hoping to spend the night and catch a dip. But asking – and extensive walking – around told me I had missed out. All accommodation closed. The beach and the front were okay but behind it was a sprawl of bucket and spade shops and rooms for rent. All closed and none of the charm I had been hoping for.

I found some grilled octopus to my liking and asked again of the waiter. They had a room above but it was expensive and they'd only rent it for a minimum of three nights. We left for Thessaloniki on a road bordered by oleanders, still in flower. What a wonderfully architectural, elegant and generous shrub. I wished we could grow them at home.

20

THESSALONIKI

A daunting mass of white buildings, going on for miles around the bay, revealed themselves as we crested a hill on the highway. Thessaloniki, Greece's second city.

Never arrive here on a Sunday afternoon. The roads were easily navigated but parking was non-existent, and many cars were double parked. Finally, a spot for Peds to rest his weary boots under a plane tree, and perhaps offer up a prayer at Agias Sofia – a famous church locally – and just across the street.

I had trouble reading the street signs, so I asked a passing and entwined couple if it was okay to park here. They seemed as confused as I was.

'I think it's ok for today, but it seems you might have to move the car on Tuesday,' said the man. 'How long are you staying?'

'I'm leaving on Tuesday,' I replied. 'But it's free to park here? I find that hard to believe.'

'Yes, it should be free but now looking again I'm not sure.'

'What could happen?'

'Well, they might issue a ticket.'
'But they won't tow it, will they?'
They both laughed.
'No, no that would be too much.'

I thanked them and got my bag from the boot. What a civilised country, I thought. Now that I was out of the car it was comfortable in the early evening. The light was lovely and bathed the pastel colours of the apartment blocks as they rose in ranks from the sea. I went in search of a cheap room and a cold beer.

◆•▶

Next morning, I popped into Agios Dimitrios, the city's largest church, set in its own square of fine white marble and fountains.

The bones of the saint lay inside a strange hexagonal booth, also built of marble. Penitents were picking out cotton buds cut in half from a big pile, dipping them in holy water and waving them at various points of reliquary around the building. One woman was kissing and kneeling and bowing at – I counted – six areas of devotion. She either had a lot of bad luck or a lot of bad habits.

There was a door into a garden, and I stepped through into a cool glade. It was only 9am but the day was clear and the sunshine already hot.

Back in the church I lit a candle and planted it in a mound of sand among the hundreds already alight. The candle tray was covered by an elaborate extractor hood.

My phoned pinged and I looked around embarrassed, I'd neglected to put it on silent. It was another email, my second in as many days. The allotments association asking owners to report any dead badgers so that they could be removed and tested for Bovine TB.

The name on my plot's shed is Ilios which is how Homer nearly always refers to Troy – by its ancient name – in the Iliad. Whenever anyone asked what it meant I was always delighted to tell them that Plot 47 was where I worked like a Trojan. Whatever that meant. Another question I wished I'd asked Mustapha Askin. But in truth I had been very lax with the weeds of late and would need to hit it with a minimum of Agent Orange when I got back.

Down the street, a shop selling knock-offs of famous paintings. Very bad ones. I'd once had a bet with a friend of mine that the Mona Lisa on display in the Louvre was a fake. The real one in a vault. I wondered if he remembered. He was very old now and lived on the ringing plains of Cambridgeshire. Too frail to travel to London and indulge in long lunches.

◆•▶

Assiduous readers will know that I am a fan of Atatürk and it turns out he was a Thessaloniki homeboy. I'd asked all sorts of passers-by and shopkeepers where his birthplace was, but nobody had ever heard of it. Not surprisingly, he's not exactly a local hero around these parts.

I finally located it. His house now part of the heavily fortified Turkish consulate here. But, sadly, closed on Mondays.

I found a bureau that would change my Turkish lira into euros so they wouldn't lose another ten points

TURKISH EMBASSY, THESSALONIKI

overnight. The woman behind the counter showed me what my TKL was now worth.

'Really?' I said. 'Is that the best you can do?'

'Yep, and I wouldn't leave it for another day. It's nose-diving right now.'

I took the cash and left with a sigh.

I walked downhill, along wide boulevards through rose gardens with fountains and past a Roman rotunda to the sea, where a superb bronze of Alexander astride a rearing horse stood. The promenade was wide and generous. Great town planning. Waterfront blocks had replaced the beautiful old stuccoed buildings lining the ancient harbour. But a few remained. The bay still guarded by the famous White Tower.

I'd wanted to see this so I had put it into Google maps. It told me it was a month's walk away. But that was the White Tower in the Tower of London. Idiot! I turned on my location. Reading the plaque outside I found that it had had exactly the same grisly uses as its northern namesake.

STATUE OF ALEXANDER THE GREAT ON THESSALONIKI WATERFRONT

Away from the harbour a small market. And then Ouzeria Lola's for pork chops and salad. Well, it was now two and I had been up since six.

On the way back I was leaning on a railing idly watching the reconstruction of the Roman forum. One of many large sites protected in the heart of the city. A workman with a big blowtorch was capping off the new pillar bases with a rubber membrane. I turned to a woman next to me and said, 'That's not how they did it in the old days.'

'Absolutely not,' she laughed.

Regan was from north of Boston and here for a medical procedure. This was her fourth visit. I wished her well. She had the look of a mid-westerner. Long hair blowing across her face as she squinted in the sunlight.

We got chatting and agreed that we were conflicted about reconstruction of ancient ruins. But I offered that so much space cordoned off for unintelligible ruins would not be good either. She said that until now, every civilisation had built on and over. Shouldn't we respectfully do the same? Who knew how far off the next apocalyptic event was. I wasn't sure but agreed that all artefacts should now be returned to stable governments that could protect them.

'Hah! Good luck with that one.'

After she left I took an ice cream across the street to a small park filled with yuccas and palm trees. It was slightly further up the hill, and I could look over the passing buses and down through the terraces to the creamy blue and glittering Med. The sun was going down fast now, and I watched as it dipped to the horizon and seemed to melt into the sea.

I'd really liked this town. It had been warm and welcoming and its scruffy parts only added to its charm. Another place that you could escape to and feel at home.

Thessaloniki. Perhaps not the most beautiful girl at the ball, but the one you would be lucky to live a life with.

21

RIDING PELION

In the morning I schlepped downwards towards the church to find Pedro. The streets were slippery after some light rain during the night, making me curl my feet to keep my espadrilles on. Unlike Edward Lear's Pobble I did have toes and was thankful that they were more or less all in working order.

Pedro was there where I had left him. Not towed, not clamped, not ticketed and not damaged. At least, no further damage.

◆◆◆

It was early, around seven. We got out of town and headed west, the mountains soon rose up steeply ahead of us. They looked to be covered with some thick, dark green moss, so uniform was the bushy covering.

Stopping at a tollbooth, a very chatty young chappy.
'Where you from?'
'London,' I replied.
'You drove all the way?'
I outlined where I'd been.

'I used to work in England – Portsmouth, then Southampton,' he said.

I said I knew both very well. And got back in my car conscious of the rush-hour traffic building up behind in my lane. Then he reached out and knocked on the passenger window. I wound it down.

'You know the Isle of Wight?'

'Yes indeed, I used to sail all around the Solent. Well, thank you. Very nice to meet you.'

'You too sir. Have a nice trip,' he turned back to his computer screen. But the barrier was still not up.

'You know Ventnor? The Spy Glass Inn?' he asked.

Sighing, I owned to many a pint of foaming ale at that hostelry.

'I don't like British beer,' he said.

I smiled and hooked my thumb at the traffic backed up behind us.

'Oh yes, sorry. I miss England,' he said and put the barrier up.

'So do I,' I shouted as we sped off.

But in truth I didn't really. This trip was going way too fast for that. And already I was thinking about my way home. I had been freewheeling so far. Never planning more than a day ahead. Now I was working back from the deadline of the return across the Channel. That felt a bit too much like work to me.

I stopped to fill up and let the guy get on with it, heading into the shop. Through the window I saw he was using a red gun from the pumps, not the usual unleaded green one. In a panic I banged on the window. He looked at me and smiled but carried on filling. I ran back to him shouting to stop.

PEDRO'S PROGRESS

ON THE PELION PENINSULAR

'What's that you're putting in?!' I shouted, grabbing the gun.

'It's 98, special, same price as 95 today.'

'Okay, but unleaded, yes?' I had visions of having to drain the tank.

'Ne, ne, ne...amolyvdos...endaxi?'

I examined the pump. It was unleaded. Why would they put a red gun on a green pump? Thank heavens! I made the gesture of a heart attack and he laughed.

'No problem my friend, we even have one hundred if you want it. But, expensive.'

Call it my imagination but Pedro seemed to scamper as we joined the motorway. I hoped the high-octane tankful wouldn't go to his head.

The mountains were close now, vertical and sheer. Very dark green with wet-looking mist on the tops. I thought we can't go over those, surely? And we didn't. Tunnel after tunnel took us under what was – I realised later – Mount Olympos. I wondered what the gods would have made of that in ancient times. Mortals burrowing roads under their sacred mound. Then under Mount Ossa, bypassing Volos and onto the Pelion Peninsula.

We missed a turning and detoured through Portaria. Heavy industry, palled with pollution and stinking to high heaven. The wide road of the town itself lined with workshops, broken cars and garbage. A very nassssty place. As Smeagol might say.

At the top of the Pagasitic Gulf (don't sound great, do it?) we turned left along a pleasant road alongside the sea.

There was nothing between us and the water, but

the cafes had boarded out from the land. The waiters nimbly negotiating the traffic. Lots of people were sitting out in the sunshine, inches above the water. It must be really sheltered here to do that. It reminded me of the Lake District, that closeness to the water and small islands in touching distance.

Now up along a winding road into the mountains. Rather like the Ardeche. In fact the whole feeling was of rural France, not the Greece that we all conjure up in our minds. The variety of Greece had been fascinating and for me – I suppose naively – unexpected and very welcome. Not like a single country at all, really.

We were very high now and I stopped to take some snaps but couldn't really capture the grandeur of it. The road had rugged rocks on one side and was cantilevered off on my side. Round and round the rugged rocks we went. Past open areas with stacked beehives.

Then diving into chestnut woods. Their spiky coverings lying in drifts across the road like piles of Tribbles. Giving way to maples and ferns, cool under the trees and away from the light. Water dripped off the mossy rocks and ran in the gutters and across the road in places.

I was looking for a guest house that Vlad had told me about, but I'd missed the turning. We had lost the signal for the satnav miles back so I retraced my steps. I had the hang of the narrow road now and when I could, looked ahead as the bends revealed themselves empty of traffic, so I could use all of the road to go fast. You probably think that's a joke in a Fiat Panda, but the second-generation Panda has such great handling that it makes roads like this fun.

Now the white line was unlooping beneath us like a long piece of spaghetti. Rocks to the right, a thousand-foot drop to the left, what a hoot.

Spotting the sign, I reversed up a bit and turned down a rough concrete road towards the sea. Slowing now to give the brakes a chance. I'd been pretty hard on them but there was no trace of fading. The track became a cobbled-together affair of rubble and infilled patches of concrete and then finally we were there.

This place was built like a small castle and my room was in one of the turrets. Opening the shutters I looked out like Rapunzel, but without the hair.

After a bit of a doze, I awoke starving, so back on the road to look for a taverna. I went for miles. Stopping and asking locals. Then, on the right-hand side, a glimpse of a tablecloth flapping in the breeze. Hard on the brakes, into reverse and, with a high-pitched whine from the gearbox, into their driveway.

The chatty waitress got me settled. I complimented her on her English and she told me that her mother had lived up in the mountains and didn't want that life for her daughters so had got them into a school that taught English. She said that when her mother got cranky, she and her sister spoke in English so their mother couldn't understand. I remembered that when they were young, my two sons had a bit of a secret dialogue going on that G and I could make neither head nor tail of.

I had the cheese rolls with tzatziki. Then a 'lamp' knuckle on a bed of beetroot puree that left shocking pink kisses on my napkin.

The phone buzzed. Allotments association again!

Gawd almighty, was this my life now?

'Just a reminder that the orchid talk will be held at the Age Concern rooms next to the Parish Council building.'

I set their email address to spam.

22

PLAIN TALES OF THE HILLS

Next morning it was overcast with rain out to sea. 'Oh no,' I thought. 'We don't like that.' I took a walk around the village. Lots of elegant and very well-maintained houses. Beautiful stone roofs and walls, some stucco. All the gates and shutters closed. Their owners back in the city for the winter.

The same old problem. Most of the locals had been made offers they couldn't refuse and their houses had been transformed into summer villas. Where once there had been an orchard with pomegranates and chickens, there was now hard-standing for a Range Rover. Vines replaced with bougainvillaeas. Tumble-down sheep folds had been mended and now held hot tubs.

A few locals were still here, including a rather unnerving man who stood all day staring out to sea. As if keeping watch for the next invasion. In fact, this part had never been invaded. Even the Turks had left these hill-dwellers to their own devices.

There was fruit on the trees, nuts on the ground and wild boar in the woods. Not a bad place to be marooned. If only for two days, in my case.

The village square held two tavernas. Both had shut only days before. On the door of one a handwritten note.

'End of season. See you in March.'

I wondered what it would be like in the summer.

◆•▶

Off and exploring then. I went back to my room to pick up the car keys. The owner's cat was asleep on my bed. I left the window ajar so he could get out and tiptoed through the doorway.

No sooner were we on the tarmac than we met a convoy of tourists coming the other way and pigging the road. Pedders held his ground and got his door mirror whacked for his bravery. 'Owwwww...!' Partially smashed but still serviceable. And lucky not to break the side window which I had – for once – left shut.

We drove onwards to Tsargarada, the most famous village around here. There was a church set in the square. Locked, but I could see Byzantine frescoes inside. Usual stuff, saints with their feet off the floor.

Next to the church, an enormous plane tree. Said to be the oldest and largest plane tree in Greece. I could believe it.

Back up the steps, some German tourists asked me where the giant plane was.

'Down those steps mate, you can't miss it. It's the size of a Jumbo Jet.'

There was one lonely and lovely little taverna. But too early for me after breakfast. The feeling of southern, rural France persisted. This could be the Ardeche.

The aforementioned breakfast had been a huge affair. Breads of all distinctions under napkins. Fruit and yoghurt. Then toast was brought. Followed by a Spanish omelette. Then a ham and cheese sandwich under cling film that I was ignoring was whisked away and returned toasted. Juice. Coffee. All this was accompanied by an intrusive and obviously over-indulged German Shepherd and the even more annoying and begging cat. Not really being a breakfast person, this slowed me up somewhat and I had

ALL OVER FOR THIS YEAR

considered returning to my room for a 9am siesta but resisted.

On the way back we detoured down to a beach. It must be a great spot in the summer and wasn't half bad now. It was a narrow and deeply rocky cove. A storm had brought in driftwood and eight-foot lengths of kelp.

I chatted to the owner of the beach bar who was loading his stock into a pick-up. He'd run a pub in Streatham 40 years ago. This was his retirement job. I couldn't work out his age but guessed he was around eighty.

Then it started to rain. Very slowly it became a crashing downpour. I ran to Peds and we scampered back up the hill to the main road. By the time we got to the top the road surface was like a torrent. Inches deep and streaming in sheets over the edge, spilling into the void.

The wipers came on for the first time. The interior steamed up for the first time. The windows were up for the first time. I put the blowers on hot to clear it.

Stopping at a lay-by we watched the lightning out to sea running horizontally through a sky of Payne's Grey.

23
VOLOS CITY

Driving back down the hills to the coast I had to pull hard on the reins. Pedders wanted to go faster.

'Whoah there, young man. We've got all day.'

We got into a rhythm on the sweeping bends and my pen – that I'd tossed into a metal travel mug – rang session bells as we leaned from side to side.

That morning I'd sent a chiding text to Vlad the Romanian dentist for recommending a place where everything was shut and the rain was falling.

'I am not responsible for the weather,' he replied,' I am only a dentist.'

Then he sent me a gif of Mr Bean laughing. He was a fan. I had already told him that while everyone outside Britain seemed to love Mr Bean, at home he was almost a national embarrassment. I took it as a gentle piss-take on his part.

◆●▶

Volos. The mythic home of Jason and his argonauts. Now a substantial university town with a port serving the islands of the Sporades.

Again, I was approving of the way they had protected the promenade from further incursions from the town's development. It meant a meeting place for the students and residents.

At the far end there were gardens and cafes under plane trees, where I had a very good coffee.

Although a nice town, most of its original buildings had been replaced with concrete blocks. A few dilapidated examples survived but there seemed no interest in recreating them with modern materials. A shame because I thought their faded belle epoque style rather easy on the eye.

Then a pink and white church in a square that looked like an advertisement for stone cladding. You could imagine it in Disney world. With a voiceover saying, 'We welcome you to ancient Thessaly.'

Volos is widely regarded for its tsipouradika where they serve a lethal kind of raki along with small plates of tapas. Tsipouradika, try saying that after you've had a few drinks.

In a kind of Jackass dare way I liked the sound of this, so I had to give it a go.

I found a likely place and the waiter asked how many bottles I wanted. He suggested two.

'Okay.'

Then he asked 'With or without anis?' Apparently one was like ouzo and the other like grappa. Having had trouble finding my socks under the bed – let alone putting them on – after previous experiences with grappa, I opted for the anis version.

The problem with this kind of drink is that, unless you keep a friendly lab rat about your person to test it, you really have no idea just how potent it is until someone turns the room through 90 degrees and you find yourself face down dribbling on the carpet.

Their tsispouri was homemade and came in miniature unmarked bottles. The bloke next to me poured his into a tumbler, added ice and topped it up with water. So, like ouzo then? I did the same.

I knew it was working when a chap with a clarinet played a tuneless warble for half a minute and then held his hand out. I gave him 50 cents to the amazement of the other tables. Perhaps they had been hoping for Stranger on the Shore?

The whole thing – eight small dishes including a kind of fridge cake dessert and a coffee – came to less than eight euros.

I decided a walk was in order to top up on supplies. Away from the waterfront, a couple of parallel streets sold everything you could wish for. And a few things you wouldn't wish on an enemy.

Call me a philistine but now provisioned with water and other essentials for the room, I dodged the Brick Making Museum, gave the exhibition of folk art a swerve and the Byzantine beaker and tile collection a miss.

24

LIP SERVICE

The next day I was out on the road at 7am. Most days I was up early and that was down to travelling alone. With a companion I'd be dragging out dinner and not getting to bed at nine as I had been doing.

Last night, there had been a new entertainment to add to the variety of bathroom experiences on this trip.

Flushing the loo, I pushed the cistern, which was not attached to the wall, and rocked it backwards. I didn't worry too much until I realised that the bottom of the cistern was only resting on the toilet bowl and not attached to that either! The result? Very wet feet and a flooded bathroom floor. Pissed off, I threw a towel at it and slammed the door.

In the morning it had mostly dried out, so I was very careful not to flush it again until all ablutions had been completed. I wasn't going to be hopping around like Jeremy Fisher.

This followed another cringeworthy experience in the afternoon, which very much tested my inner stoic.

The windy days had given me chapped lips, so I added lip balm to my mental shopping list. The pharmacy had some but it was ten euros. I couldn't find any in the mini market so I asked the girl at the checkout using Google translate. She reached above her counter and showed me some.

'We only have this, but it is Cola,' making to put it back. I gestured that was okay and I would buy it.

'You still want it?' she said. I nodded and she looked at me dubiously as she bagged it.

I put it on in the street. Silly girl, I thought to myself, that's Cherry not Cola. But on returning to my room, I looked at myself in the mirror to discover I had bright pink lips. She hadn't said cola – she had said coloured! Not so silly after all.

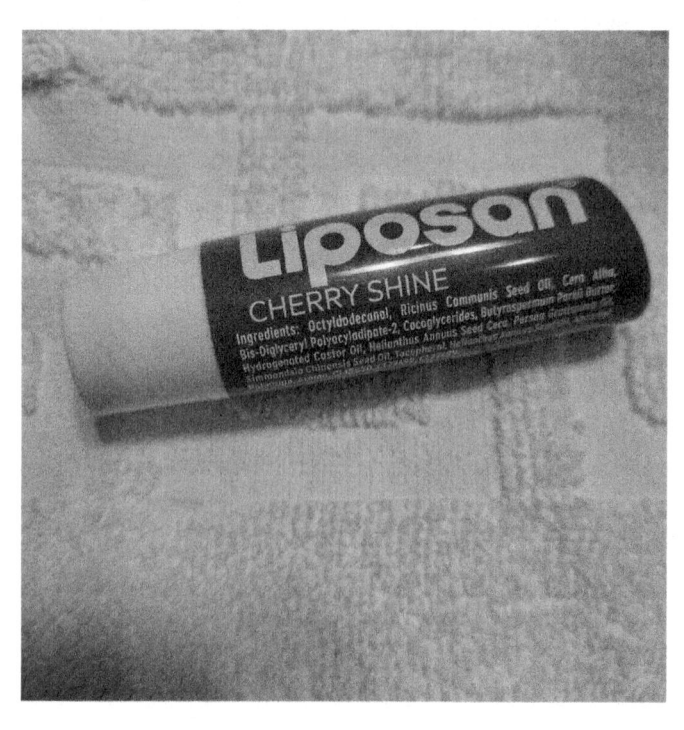

LIP SERVICE

All day long I'd been applying this stuff and it had been working well. I'd been smiling at waitresses and chatting to people in the street made up like Widow Twankey. One man in the supermarket had goggled at me.

<•>

We drove out of town and once inland the clouds disappeared. We travelled along A roads. But you could see bits and pieces of the new highway in the making. A bridge to nowhere. A newly graded slope.

Then police had blocked the highway. Out of a dusty side road appeared big military trucks with serious-looking rocket launchers. Sabre rattling from Turkey was being ramped up. More hard-man politics. The news was full of it. I hadn't really watched TV here but you would see it in the cafes and bars.

This was an empty landscape of domed hills. A quarry here, a solar farm there, but lonely. Good horse-riding country. I spotted a shepherd, leading his horse with its wooden saddle. After a couple of hours of bowling along mostly empty roads we came to the start of the Meteoran rock formations. Like something out of a John Ford movie set in Monument Valley. Huge and impressively vertiginous pillars of rock that had been created over the millennia.

Ten million years ago, the tops of those rocks had been the bed of an inland sea. According to my guidebook, over thousands of years erosion had sculpted the landscape into towers of rock, laced with caves, in hermit monks holed up. Of the 24 monastries established on these impossible peaks, six are open to visitors.

The name Meteora means suspended in the air. These monasteries are the closest thing to their Tibetan equivalent as you can get. I decided that I would have to take a look. The day hot under a Swiss chalet sky.

What to say about Meteora? It's a kind of ridiculous place really. Heavily curated and with a tour bus herding instinct. I thought the geography looked a lot more interesting than the monasteries but visited two of them anyway.

Originally, they were reached via ladders made of olive wood that could be rolled up. And later windlass and pulleys allowed pilgrims to be pulled up in nets.

James Bond had climbed up one of these in the film 'For Your Eyes Only'. Roger Moore hand over hand, up a rope in a polo-neck sweater with a Magnum .44 in a shoulder holster. 'Oooh Jemms...!' You could not possibly have done that. The sandstone rock face was sheer and wider at the top than the bottom. Joe Simpson himself would have lit a cigarette and walked away.

Anyway, why bother when there's a road to the top? Well, almost. At Agios Stefanos you walk up a paved path for a kilometre to a miniature doorway and then along an open passage cut into the rock. All very Lord of the Rings.

At the monastery itself there were fit Norwegians carrying babies, and elderly – but spry – American ladies with scrambling boots on their bone-thin ankles.

I thought how much G would have loved it. Just her cuppa. But any expectation of a religious experience was nullified by loud voices comparing numbers of steps gathered on Apple watches.

Down below, in the village of Kastraki (an unfortunate name for the local menfolk), the scale felt imposing but safe. After all, it had taken ten million years to get to this point. No boulder was about to take out the town, hopefully. But because the rocks had been gently rounded by the elements over millennia, it was very hard to get any sort of handle on their scale. They looked like children's toy bricks placed by a giant.

I settled down in the shade with a beer – at what turned out to be a very good restaurant – and tried to gather my thoughts. Then a good-looking girl strode in and the two – previously chatty – waiters went into freeze frame. She marched straight to the owner who was sitting like Jabba the Hutt with prayer beads in the dark interior. A hasty negotiation took place. An inclined head from him was all she needed and almost immediately a gaggle of 20 Brits arrived for lunch. They faffed and fussed about where to sit. Then made bad calls on what to eat. Soups and salads and bottles of water. I thought, why even bother? Their conversation evasive and lumpen.

I ordered the very fine pork chops and chatted in schoolboy Italian to my neighbouring table. A couple from just south of Venice. They were – I guessed – in their seventies, and still very much in love. She wagged fingers at him, and he made her giggle back.

Life is sweet, as they say.

25

NORTH BY NORTHWEST

Meteora was one of those places you just had to see if you were passing. So now I'd been there and done that. A very comfortable night in the best room so far. Doupiani House had all the charm of a tea planter's residence in the high country. And importantly, everything was bolted down in the bathroom.

I'd opened the doors and shutters and a cool breeze coming off the mountain should have meant a peaceful night. However, I was restless because I was now at a crossroads in my journey. I had to decide whether to go north and through North Macedonia, Albania, Montenegro, Croatia and Slovenia. Or go northwest, across to Italy, then Sicily, Sardinia and Corsica to France.

I plumped for the latter because it kept me south for longer and because it was full of stuff that I wanted to see and do. An indulgence then but sights and sounds that G was less likely to find interesting or would be able to leave her job long enough for.

Logistically it was a lot more complicated and probably more expensive, with all the ferry connections.

But it was less of a tourist trap and avoided that boring journey across the top of Italy. Lake Bled and the Dalmatian Coast would have to wait. In truth they just didn't speak to me like the other route, so I left the Balkans guide book in the room and shouldered my bag to Pedders.

A bright and chilly morning. I could see my breath. A good-to-be-alive day. What day wasn't? But this morning it was so obvious that even a chronic curmudgeon would be charmed.

A super road led up into the mountains and then down the other side across bridges and through tunnels to Igoumenitsa. Some of the tunnels were six kilometres long. Try holding your breath all the way through those, kids!

About 30 kilometres outside the port I could smell the sea. And soon it came into view. A beautiful natural bay flanked by pretty islands and headland.

LORRY DRIVERS, IGOUMENETSIA PORT

I got to the port where giant wind turbine rotor blades were being craned aboard a freighter. I checked in and went in search of a coffee. The ferry to Bari didn't leave until midnight. I needn't have got up quite so early. But it was a lovely day, after all. The cafe had an interesting picture of the port from 1954. Not a lot had changed except for the scale and, of course, the ubiquitous concrete. The picture showed a charabanc driving onto what looked like a landing craft, while the passengers stood around watching. The men in astrakhan hats as the women bought pretzels from a street vendor in a white coat.

<•>

Finally we got through customs. It had been thorough and tense. Pedders lost his modesty.

'Well really… you want to look up that pipe..? You might have warmed your hands first.'

I had been told to go to gate ten but had no idea where that could be. The apron was massive, miles long. I met some truck drivers having a salad and a few rakis and they handed me a glass of the firewater neat.

Naturally, with so much acreage to play with. Nobody really knew where to park apart from the truck drivers. Or indeed where to drive. I saw several scrapes and small accidents as car drivers appeared through ranked columns of container lorries. Not knowing who had the right of way.

There was a rig parked next to me with the name 'Breeders: Danish Genetics' and a picture of a flying pig on the side. What the hell? On my other side, a leaking refrigerated truck blocking me in with a strong smell of rotten fish. I took a walk and chatted to some Italians exercising their dogs.

A chap on a big Honda drew up in front of me, took off his helmet and shook out his long grey hair. He was a Belgian called Guy. We exchanged a few words and then he went off for a pee. Then I was joined by a lady who had parked her rust-red motorhome behind me. We stood looking out to sea for the arrival of the ferry but all was black against the glare from the floodlights.

'Come on,' she said. 'Enough of this. I've got a good bottle of wine in the van.'

So, I followed her inside which was pretty messy.

'Excuse all this,' she said, dumping a basket of washing onto the bed to make room at the table. 'When you travel alone you stop clearing up after a while.'

I opened the wine, a Bulgarian red, while she rinsed a couple of stubby tumblers in the sink.

'How long have you been travelling?' I asked.

'About eight months in total, but I spent six months of that in Iran.'

Blimey, I thought. A lone woman in Iran. Intrepid. She then went on to tell me that she was Dutch but was travelling back to Marseille where a friend had some horse stables. She would leave the van there and fly to Lanzarote where she owned a house for the winter. She had blonde hair cut short and badly. I wondered if she'd cut it herself. And a ruddy, weather-beaten face. I put her in her mid-seventies.

'Do you mind if I ask how old you are?'

'Take a guess,' she said.

'Please don't be offended but I'd say seventy-four.'
'Not offended at all,' she said. 'I'm ninety-seven!'
'Good god!' I laughed. 'That's amazing.'

I thought how I'd decided to do this trip before I got too old to do so. I hoped I'd have the guts to do it at her age.

◆•▶

On board the ferry there was no room at the inn. Correction, there was one cabin that the purser wanted 198 euros for. This was a relatively short hop across to Bari so I went in search of somewhere to bunk down. The time was now 2am and I was tired.

Old hands on this route had brought along duvets and double mattresses which they set up in stairwells and bar areas. One enterprising couple had even pitched a two-man tent on deck. I went back to the reception and the bloke at the desk must have felt pity for me. He offered a free couchette.

I was directed to my seat in the pitch-dark compartment by a crew member with a torch, just like an usher in a cinema. The seat stank and was rough like a bristly doormat. I put my head back and tried to ignore it. The experience that night was the equivalent of sleeping over your cattle in a medieval farmhouse. The lowing of the other passengers with strange smells, cries and snorts.

26
PIZZO MY HEART

THE PROM AT PIZZO

It's never a good idea to arrive anywhere on a Sunday. Especially in a Catholic country. The world and his wife were out and about in the beautiful little town of Pizzo on the instep of Italy, the northern coast of Calabria.

Pedro squeezed – with millimetres to spare – between two large Mercs parked at right angles to each other in a corner at the beach car park.

'Sono proprio stanco!' he admitted.

And I agreed. I was cream crackered and hadn't really slept for 48 hours, during which the driving had added up to around 600 miles. I'd had to force myself to stop at one point when I came close to the crash barrier on a couple of occasions. Driving with your eyes shut is never a good idea. But, as the joke goes, the only way to drive in Italy.

Pizzo is one of a string of pearls down this coastline which include Tropea and Scylla. A great place to tour as there are airports at Reggio in the toe and Terme in the ankle. Next time you have a week to spare, get a one-way hire car and give it a go.

I had first visited Pizzo a few years before with my leg in a brace and had second thoughts about its verticality. Now I noticed there were tuk-tuks to take you from the main square at the top to the lower town on the beach, which was where I was staying.

◄•►

That morning, waiting to disembark the boat at Bari, I got chatting to Guy, the rider of the Honda I'd met on the dock the previous evening. He was from Brussels and was making his way home too, after about six weeks in Greece. I told him that I was heading back and about the route I had chosen.

He said he didn't like the Balkans much. Especially Serbia, where he'd felt distinctly unwelcome. I'd just watched a documentary about how the First World War started and I could imagine there was still a lot of resentment on many counts.

An interesting man. He'd introduced supermarkets into Côte D'Ivoire and later to Romania after the regime changed.

'Ex-Stasi guys would flock in and fill the boots of their Mercedes. But it was the ordinary people that would queue and buy just a small bar of high-quality soap, that really got me. They wanted a piece of the West. But that was all they could afford.'

He said that Romania was one of the most beautiful countries he'd ever known and the people also. I wondered if a certain Bucharest dentist's ears were burning.

◂•▸

Pizzo was a gorgeous place to slob out for a couple of days. Basically, I just dossed around and topped up the tan. Aurelio at the little restaurant up the road would serve me a superb octopus salad and a glass of white wine. And in the evenings I drank Campari Spritz and watched the comings and goings of the locals. I got my washing done with the help of Gabriela who laughed at me because I couldn't work out the washing machine.

'Dio mio!' she said

HAPPY IN HIS SKIN. WAITER IN PIZZO

And I should have gone in the sea but it was starting to rain and I didn't fancy it. Forse domani?

◆•▶

That evening the town was dead. I grabbed an umbrella from Pedders and scampered up the steps to the main square. Not a lot doing at the cafes. The waiters, wrong-footed by the rain twice, were weary of clearing the tables and mopping down seat cushions.

I went into a church and found a saint with my daughter's name. Saint Anna looked disapproving of her cherub's dirty dress.

Then I found a pizza joint. The waiters playing video games. I woke them up and ordered an nduja pizza made with the local spicy sausage. It was brilliant.

In my experience that is Italy all over. The food is either fantastic or bloody dreadful. You can never tell by the outside. Or by the presentation on the inside. But somewhere, buried in a very hot basement, is a chef who either knows what he or she is doing, or not.

Whatever, you are always guaranteed a welcome if you try a bit of charm. I really got to like the guys here. The joint had the feeling of a London pub during a train strike. The rain outside now coming down hard. Everyone sequestered in the comradeship of a lock-in. The waiter, a table of Swedes, a local B&B owner and me. Good fun.

The waiter showed me pictures on his phone of his local exploits to expand his waistline. Including porchetta – slow roasted pork shoulder – for breakfast. It looked great and I thought how I would get up early for that.

When I was leaving I went over to the four Swedes. They were ABBA lookalikes. Very healthy.

'Where are you from?' I didn't want to guess but I was sure they were Swedish.

'Sweden!' they chorused.

I told them I had guessed that because I'd watched a lot of Wallander. And they all roared with laughter and invited me for a drink.

'Do you like Scotch whisky?'

'I do, I do, I do, I do, I do…!' I sang to them.

27
SWEET SICILIA

Last night, sleeping with the doors open, a spectacular lightning show out at sea. And later, a cloudburst and another massive drenching. Rain pouring off the cliffs like a waterfall from the higher town. That was around 3am.

In the morning, a lollipop-swivelling Kojak was on the TV. It suited him being dubbed into Italian.

'Chi ti ama tesora?' he asked.

Humid as hell. I threw on some trunks and then threw myself into the sea. Gorgeous.

Afterwards, I put my towel on the car seat and drove out of Dodge bare-chested and bare-footed, feeling quite the libertine and passing Italian pedestrians already wearing their overcoats.

Up past the stone fort on the belvedere whose dungeons held grey, shop window manikins wearing raggedy clothes to look like prisoners. Apparently, its claim to fame is that the execution of Napoleon's brother was held there.

I easily found the short-hop ferry from Reggio to Messina. I chatted away to Brendon. He was from

BLUFERRIES
GRUPPO FERROVIE DELLO STATO ITALIANE
IMBARCO
SICILIA
BLUFERRIES
TICKET OFFICE

Brighton and travelling on his motorbike. His neighbours were completely redoing their house so they asked if they could rent his for six months. He'd been round Ireland. Then two months in Italy. Next, he was off for three months in a motorhome around New Zealand. He was 76 years old.

'I love travelling,' he said. 'But I also love to come home. I think England is the best place to live in the world.'

I agreed. But added that I hadn't travelled that much.

'What do you love about it?' he said.

I thought for a bit.

'The humour. The seasons. No heavy-handed state intervention. Police without guns. The Chiltern Hills and Brakspear's bitter.'

'And top of that list is my wife and our children. That goes without saying.'

He nodded.

'A good list. And good enough for our short lifetime.' He smiled and I could see his Irish charm shine through.

◆•▸

The port road was a joke. Potholes worthy of the Sea of Tranquility. Any of them were enough to break a leg on my donkey. Grounding-deep and sharp-edged. Pedro treated them warily.

Then on the highway, OMG! A half-arsed contraflow. 130kph down to zero with no warning, then a left-hander at right-angles. On the return to our side of the road a big new white Tesla had managed the right turn but the driver must have lost it by overcorrecting. He'd landed on top of the crash barrier. Good shot! That was going to be expensive.

While we crawled by – very slowly – I saw the owner remonstrating with the highway maintenance crew as they used a digger to push the car back onto the road. But only managing to tear a wheel off. The owner jumping up and down now in such exasperation it was comical. Perhaps he was regretting texting his mistress at the wheel and saying that he was going to be late? Now he wasn't going to come at all.

‹•›

BAR OWNER – SAVERIO

In Catania I had arrived just in time for lunch at the fish market. I settled down to watch the antics of the traders over some very fresh prawns and a glass of Etna bianco.

The heart of this city is mostly Baroque, style-wise. This is the Spanish influence and belies their oppression of the local population into serfdom. It's impressive but also kind of fake in a show-offish filmset kind of way, and typically this is what every tourist takes pictures of.

While I was contemplating the beauty of the main square I actually heard a tourist say:

'Lookit here..I just done took a pitcher of it.'

For me though, the reality and the value of Italian towns is – nearly always – away from the old town and in the back streets. It can be pretty hit or miss. But it's something that calls me and makes me get the phone out to snap it. When you find it you know everything, the history is revealed. Fading stucco, revealed brickwork, haphazard exterior plumbing all lends to its charm.

The nearest thing I've found in describing it is Japanese Wabi Sabi. The reveration of a pot that has not fired properly or in minor imperfections in almost any object. It makes it personal to you and worthless to others.

That night I went to a local restaurant Saverio had recommended. He ran the bar down the street and had helped me out with parking.

I had the grilled octopus on a potato mousse. And after, sautéed clams and mussels. The best meal of the trip so far. There was the tiniest hint of thyme in with the mussels, wine and parsley. Perfetto!

I had a nightcap with Saverio. Really getting into

my stride now! He gave me some of the chocolate he was eating.

'Try this. It's Sicilian. I love it.'

It was that grainy stuff they produce in Modica. But it had a flavour I couldn't place.

'It's a strange flavour, no? Marijuana,' he said, and went back to the bar.

'What..?!' I said, already laughing.

A guy on a neighbouring table said, 'Don't worry. He means marjoram.'

But in truth I wasn't sure!

28

EUREKA

The day started well. On the way to Syracuse we decided on a giro of Etna. We climbed for about an hour. Then the mist cleared and we started to go through pretty towns north of Catania, built in the Genoese style. Plant life was lush. With palms, vines and umbrella pines. Every railing covered with the exotic purple of convolvulus.

Then, glimpses of the caldera through gaps in the trees and old lava flows. Mountainous, bald terrain with snow on the tops.

We got as high as we could and turned around in the mostly deserted coach park. Then we were on our way down again. Past black and yellow snow markers and a snow cat parked under a wooden shelter. Ears popping, we followed the road downwards and then…

'What the flip?!'

A warning light in the shape of an orange engine appeared on the dash. We stopped and I went to the boot to find the manual.

It said it was an ignition or fuel supply issue and to consult a Fiat agent. 'Damn!' But it also said it would be OK to drive.

'Alrighty then! Onwards, Pedro.'

I slammed the boot and thought I'd just take a look under the bonnet. As I went to the passenger door for the release catch I saw the front left wheel trim lying flat on the road. There was a smell of burning plastic. I couldn't work it out at first because these trims are held on by the wheel bolts. Then I realised that the wheels must have got so hot the holes had melted around the bolts and when we stopped the trim had just flopped off. It had only been held there by centrifugal force.

I went round the other side. Same thing. Bizarre! The wheel trim simply lying by the wheel on the road. Molten plastic dripping off the wheel bolts. I was tempted to touch it. In the way that you do in an Indian restaurant when the waiter says, 'Be careful sir. Plate is very hot.'

But Pedro shook his head.

What could it be? Brakes binding? I didn't think I had been using the brakes overly hard. Hmmm, no clue. Pedro was silent on the matter. The automotive equivalent of a donkey nibbling on a patch of wayside grass.

Under the bonnet all was normal. Oil okay. Water okay. The gauge said water temperature okay too. On we went.

◂•▸

Now, what should have been a pretty drive, was marred by garbage. We passed the towns of Randazzo and Bronte – with its connection to Horatio Nelson. The

Dukedom of Bronte was granted to Nelson by Ferdinand III, King of Sicily, in gratitude for protecting the island from the revolutionary French. But every lay-by had rubbish piled in it. Some of it had clearly been there for weeks. A mafia thing I guessed. I'd read that waste disposal was something they liked to control because it could so quickly become a local election issue if not sorted out. In other words, payments made.

On the outskirts of Syracuse, we popped into a Fiat agent and they immediately rigged Peds up to a computer. Imagine getting that service at home. They thought it was a coolant issue but weren't sure. Could I pop back tomorrow when their auto electrician was in?

◆◆◆

Ortigia is the fortified peninsula attached to Syracuse by a bridge. Its famous son was Archimedes. When the Romans invaded, Marcellus, the general in charge, issued orders to find and detain him. But Archimedes, hearing banging on his door, answered sword in hand and was promptly run through by a centurion. No extra bag of salt for that soldier, I guessed.

You can drive into it but much of it is covered by a ZTL. Many historic towns in Italy are subject to Zona Traffico Limitato. Only at certain times of the day are you allowed access and then only for loading. So, we parked up and I did the rest on foot. Now I was glad I'd brought my folding wheels because the backpack was heavy and the day sunny, with high humidity.

SYRACUSE'S FAMOUS SON – ARCHIMEDES

Got to my room, a lot of stairs up but worth it for the views afforded from my balcony. I ran a glass of water and looked out at the beautiful afternoon of clear blue skies. The wind had freshened and rain was forecast, but I couldn't see it happening right now.

29
IN DOCK

Next morning, I dropped Pedro off at the dealership. Francesco, a very handsome young man, took down some details. Passport photographed, address in Sicily, home address, telephone number, email address and then National Insurance number. Luckily, I managed to find that on my phone because – he said – he absolutely could not proceed without it.

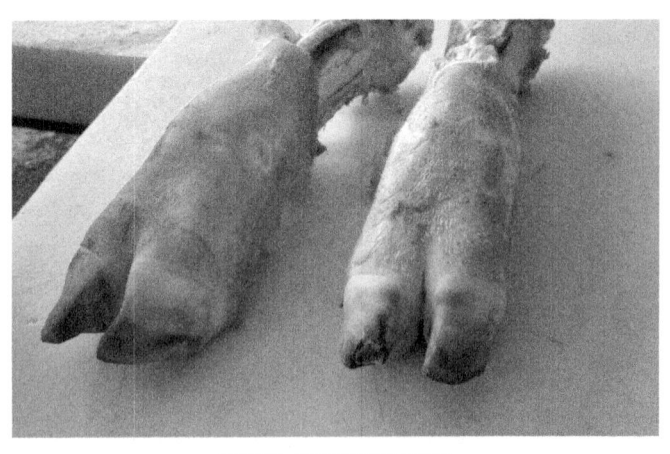

HURRY, ONLY TWO LEFT!

Walking back, I found a market. A proper one. Fabulous vegetables. And fish. Everything looked amazing. Even the celery. And all very cheap. You could live well here. I saw some very small pears. The trader told me he only sold by the kilo. Okay, I said. The price was a euro fifty.

I stuck to the lungomare, the walled walkway where the island met the sea. Some nice buildings with even better views. All a little down at heel in that relaxed Italian fashion.

It was amazing to contemplate that Syracuse was once the most important town in the whole of Magna Graecia. Even the Romans paid their dues. Until Hannibal and his Carthaginians showed up and they changed their allegiance.

Back in Ortigia I spent some time in Piazza del Duomo. What a square! It is something to behold. Beautiful, elegant, an absolute knockout. One to rival San Marco. It has a human scale and a perfection of colour that makes that severe Venetian piazza look stiff and cold by comparison. And that's from a massive Venice fanboy.

The cathedral itself has a stunning Baroque façade and, set within the portico, a pair of very fine Solomonic columns. But inside it has a kind of homeliness and rustic rough stonework of the original temple. You can see the huge Doric columns that were infilled with stone blocks after an earthquake weakened the structure. It's a very impressive building.

Round the corner was the Archimedes Museum One for the kids really, with lots of hands-on stuff, but informative.

Archimedes truly was amazing. His eureka bath

moment. Machines for flinging gigantic stone blocks and mirrors for burning ships. Pulley systems that let a single man winch a trireme onto a dry dock. Pi or 3.142. And of course, his screw for irrigation.

I read a quote by Plutarch that summed it up. And Plutarch was no slouch, either.

'It is not possible to find in geometry more profound and difficult questions treated in simpler and purer terms. For no one could by his own efforts discover the proof, and yet as soon as he learns it from him, he thinks he might have discovered it himself.'

Outside and round a corner, a motorcyclist carrying his helmet. It was Brendan! Amazing! He was just leaving for Catania.

We sat down for a natter and I told him all about Pedro. He'd seen the Tesla incident too and it unnerved him how closely the cars and trucks followed behind. We swapped numbers and wished each other safe travels.

'Maybe see you in Palermo,' he said as he got on his bike.

As I got back to my room, clouds quickly gathered. A lot of rain then ensued on my balcony, so I holed up watching the lightning. A big three-masted barque was putting out to sea, disappearing into the low cloud. What a lovely room I'd snagged here. And to be marooned for an extra night was no hardship.

By 5pm I'd heard nothing from Francesco. Nobody was picking up the phone at the dealership. So, I got in a cab and went to see what was cooking.

'You need a new transmitter. We have ordered one, but it won't be here this week.'

IN DOCK

COLUMN DETAIL, MONREALE

Today was Thursday. I had a ferry crossing to Sardinia on Sunday.

'When next week?' I asked.

He shrugged. 'Next week. You can take the car and drive short distances.'

'What about as far as Palermo?'

'I advise not.'

'What might happen if I do?'

'The problem is a coolant temperature transmitter. It could mean the car might overheat and stop the engine.'

'I see, like a sensor? Fine, give me the part number and I'll try to pick one up en route.'

'Certo.'

'What about the brakes? You know the wheel trims melted off?'

He put his hands out, palms upturned, pursed his lips and closed his eyes. 'Not a problem.'

'Really? Okay sod it. No risk, no fun.' This last bit I muttered to myself but he overheard.

'Giusto.' he said, looking at me in that sad Italian way. God, he was going to break some hearts. Not least his mother's.

◆•▶

Next morning, a clear and fresh day. Beautiful sunlight on the buildings. We ignored Francesco's advice and got on the road to Palermo. With everything crossed.

The road goes cross country. Past the mountain-top towns of Enna and Caltinesetta. Over roads on stilts above marshes. Prickly pear, everywhere.

Then into some tunnels so badly lit it felt like we were inside a coal mine. On the other side of the mountains, as we came out of the final tunnel, heavy rain. The wipers could barely cope. Then flying through the outskirts of Palermo. Dicing with the mid-morning traffic, the mad filtering of roads – making for split-second judgements – and the potholes, naturally.

I thought we'd make a quick pitstop at Monreale. A cathedral on a hill in a suburb of Palermo. A long history entangled with Arab invasion and later Norman patronage, it has a reputation for its mosaics.

The main apse is huge and very high. Then a series of side chapels. All very ornate. Some people go crazy for this stuff, but it wasn't the kind of sacred architecture I rated that highly. I'd paid 13 euros and had spent about the same number of minutes inside. Some nice bronze doors by Pisano featuring relief scenes from the Old Testament, I spent quite a few minutes looking at those.

Back in Palermo I found a parking garage and went to the hotel. All I could find was a tenth-floor bar with the same name and that was shut. There was a great view through the locked glass doors. I called them up and they said they would meet me there. The rooms were on the same floor.

It was all a bit like a hostel but organised and clean. I just hoped the two-person lift didn't break down, I didn't fancy the stairs. I headed out for a walk.

I found Palermo as annoying as I had on previous occasions. Hard-nosed and everyone on the make. It just lacks charm for me and although it's right on the coast, there are no views of the sea. A squint down a boulevard reveals that someone has parked a cruise ship across it.

I found a fish joint at the end of the famous Vucceria market. I was here five years ago and it is almost a joke that this market is so revered and signposted when it is but a shadow of its former self. The food was fine, but it was all plastic glasses and cutlery and twice the price of Catania.

I thought to myself, 'I'm not sure I can spend another day here.' But Pedders needed rest and was blocked in the underground parking until Sunday.

30
DAYTRIPPER

Whoever in their wisdom had decided to replace the door handles inside this hotel's rooms with push bars needed to have his head examined.

If you wanted to lock your door you had to do it from outside. Then you slammed it shut. Pressing the bar to exit like a fire door to the street in a theatre. They must have found these doors cheap somewhere because even the bathroom had one. Nasty.

In said bathroom, the very bright lights and very noisy fan worked on a proximity sensor. So, popping in there during the night was a proper wake up call. I tried to play statues but there was no escaping it. And then of course, the fact that the hotel had no street entrance apart from a tiny lift to the tenth floor 'Sky Bar'. Which was closed at night.

I'd asked the owner to print my ferry tickets and he begrudgingly agreed. I emailed them to him, and he'd hand cranked his ancient computer into action. By nightfall it had finished updating and the printer smoked into life.

Although I'd pointed out that I only needed pages 1 and 3 containing the barcodes, he printed all eight pages including the terms and conditions and had somehow also managed to print four copies. He was rather dismayed as he handed over a small telephone book of A4 paper.

'You give hotel 5-star review, I hope?' he asked.

Hmmm... not sure.

◆•▶

PRETTY MONDELLO

At 4am there was a big row from the French couple in the room next door. The word *putain* came through loud and clear. This was then followed by a lot of hissed murmuring. Then headboard banging for what seemed like 20 minutes. But we men are never good at gauging time in such situations. Then quiet. Either they had made up big time or he had brained her against the bed rail. I wasn't particularly bothered either way.

◆•▸

It had rained a lot in the night. But it had also rained in my room. The air conditioning unit had dripped water over my passport and money. Also the ferry tickets, which I carefully peeled apart and laid out on the bed to dry. I couldn't face the owner having to print them again.

Streetside, there was a smell of fishy sewers. Lovely! Palermo I am trying to love you but you won't love me back. I made my way skipping puddles – and dodging a drowning from passing cars. The bus stop was quite a hike. If I'd had the nous I would have taken a bus to get there. But information was non-existent.

The 806 was like something out of Harry Potter. It fairly hacked along reaching speeds of around 60 mph and showering pedestrians in muddy water from the puddles. In about 30 minutes and for just €1.40, we reached the seaside town of Mondello. It was early and I had arrived with the help.

A very pretty place with little painted fishing boats and clear waters. A sandy beach with a small casino and funfair.

Lowering clouds made me take shelter in a café where two very good coffees were consumed. And also, where I was bitten several times by mosquitoes. They too were trying to keep out of the rain. Then it brightened and I thought, I've got a chance of a decent day at the beach.

I was about to negotiate a bed and brolly deal when the heavens opened, the rain apparently falling from a cloudless sky. I was forced back under an awning. It really set in now and I was getting soaked. The bus was approaching on the other side of the street, so I hailed the driver and he stopped.

Back in the smoke, I paid a visit to Pedro to get a change of footwear. He was behind six lines of cars at the very back. I must have looked a little dismayed because the attendant was at pains to assure me that by tomorrow morning Pedro would be at the front.

In search of lunch, I found an unassuming and totally brilliant trattoria curiously called La Gondola. I had fettuccine with a thick seafood ragu, prawns and pistachios. Superb. At the next table were two girls and a guy from Hannover. They were here for the football game. I wished them good luck.

'We love London. We know all the Weatherspoons!'

Just outside the restaurant I spotted a cousin of Pedro's. A Panda of a similar age and colour but now a dusty pink. So, this is what he would look like once he'd lost all his varnish?

31

PER SARDINIA

Pedro was chafing at the bit.
'Tranquilo bello, it's only a short run downhill to the port.'

Hannover 86 had beaten Palermo 4-1. I wondered how my German friends' heads would be feeling when they woke up?

One more thing about the motion sensor in the bathroom. When you were behind the shower curtain… guess what? Yep, the sensor couldn't detect any motion and promptly left you in the dark. And sitting still on the loo? Well, one could go on.

The town was quiet for once. Just the cicada sound the traffic lights make when it's safe to cross. But what if there was an actual cicada sitting on the traffic light? Dodgy for the visually impaired.

Outside the Grand Hotel, four very beautiful 488 Ferraris were parked up with rally numbers on their doors. Not a squashed fly on their bonnets yet.

I woke the sleeping parking attendant and rolled the lil' donkey to the port where the gates were shut. I had been warned to arrive early as this was a popular route

FERRY TO SARDINIA

and the only one for a week. The hotel owner had said that even with a ticket you could get bumped.

Eventually someone opened the gate and directed me to another entrance down the road. This was very much a commercial port and huge. I had to stop and ask directions several times. After a couple of kilometres dodging the usual craters I found the ship. A big lad.

Pedders had a grand view for once from the open-air car deck. But getting there was hairy. We went up a steep and slippery steel ramp.

Egged on by the deck capo I made the mistake of following the car in front too closely. When he got to the top the idiot driver stopped to have a look around. Oblivious that someone might be behind him. Brilliant. if anything was going to test the clutch this would. And no weight on the front wheels.

But he was the one with the problem. He stalled his ancient Passat. Then ordered everyone out. Four big people exited and shuffled along the edges of the ramp clinging to the car's roof bars. The deckhand came and chocked his wheels.

'Hmmm,' I thought.

Pedders rolled defensively back down the ramp. Passat man restarted the engine and tried to climb but instead went backwards, straight over the wheel chocks towards me.

'Double shit!' I said out loud.

Finally, his handbrake held and he stopped a few inches from my bumper. OMG that could have been curtains for Pedro. I was furious.

I waved both arms out the window helplessly to the crewman and he stopped all traffic behind us and raised the ramp to horizontal. Now we were suspended in the air on a plate of steel several metres up in the air with nothing behind us.

He tiptoed down like a tightrope walker and said with a grin.

'Sempre dritto. D'accordo?' I understood alright. But spotting my plates he said, 'We only go forward now. Agreed?'

'Totally, dude!' I warbled, which made him laugh.

Finally, parked on deck, I approached the Passat driver and his passengers. He looked a bit defensive until I told him he'd left his lights on.

At the last minute I had upgraded my ticket and got the Francis Drake suite for only £17. Shouldn't that be Sir Francis? Very nice double bed and lounge with portholes, one of which looked out to starboard under the bridge wing. The other was just below the bridge, giving me the captain's eye view. Not bad accommodation. Especially as this line took a dim view of putting up your tent on deck. There were 'NO CAMPING' signs all over the ship.

NO HAPPY CAMPERS ON THIS BOAT!

I went out on deck and looked down at the water far below. Just as we passed beyond the harbour wall. Three men in a boat no more than ten feet long were fishing. They were very closely alongside and an inbound container ship on their other side. Madness. They were so vulnerable. Only on a brilliant clear day like this could you get away with it without being run down. As I watched they were hit by the combined wakes of these two towering ships and they clung to the sides in consternation.

Slowly, much more slowly than the bus it seemed, we passed Mondello where I'd had my abortive beach trip. The weather now hopefully set fair. We rounded the western cape of the island before turning north. I always think of Corsica, Sardinia and Sicily stacked vertically above each other, but they're not. And here we were closer to – and on the same latitude as – Tunis than Cagliari in Sardinia, where we were headed.

32

CAGLIARI KICK BACK

We docked late at Cagliari. I dumped the car and hoofed it to a little hotel I'd found on the way.

The next morning, driving around to different places to see if I could get this sensor swapped out on Pedro resulted in a negative. Language problems and general disinterest. Who could blame them? It was Monday morning.

The traffic was fluid and good fun. A bit like the dodgems.

Back at the hotel I bemoaned my plight to Luca at reception. He took all the details and said he'd phone around.

I walked up past the old town to the belvedere where a glorious morning awaited me. The caramel-coloured stones of old Cagliari resplendent in the morning sun. After a stiff climb I came to the Bastione di Saint Remy, a monumental neoclassical wall with twin staircases. At the top, a wide and empty plaza. The walls at the end provided some deep shade which was welcome. Despite sunscreen and straw hat, my head was starting to cook.

Looking out over the sweep of the bay I could see that my boat was still in harbour.

This place is very steep and it was kind of cool that the local corporation had installed rather stylish glass lifts all over this part of town.

The church of Santa Maria, high up on the hill, has some ornate crypts, and I spent 20 minutes or so studying their baroque decoration, until the heat drove me back outside. Another candle for our dead cat. I hoped it was working. It was costing me a small fortune. And meant that I never had any tipping *spicoli*.

The archaeological museum, which was excavated from under a church, was all a bit dusty and boring but the way they had set a floating walkway all the way around, over the unearthed Roman streets, was impressive.

THE BELVEDERE ABOVE CAGLIARI TOWN

Coming down through the back streets I bought a few bits of witty postcard art from Fabrizio Antonio Ibbo, who treated me to an excellent coffee in his studio at the back of his shop. No luck yet about the car part, said a text from Luca, so I headed to the beach.

◆•▶

The drive out to Poetto Beach – which is backed by a lagoon covered in flamingos – was very hot. I parked up under some pines and next to the spitting image of Pedro. This car had exactly the same paint problems. I thought, how hard can getting this part be? There were bazillions of these Pandas around. As I pondered, a text came through from Luca. He had found the sensor. Now I just had to get it fitted.

On the strand the wind was blowing a force-eight gale. The kite surfers were having a great time out in the bay. This is where they hold heats for America's Cup yachts.

The first place I came to wanted €28 for a bed for four hours.

'Hmmm… not sure.'

The next place said I could have a deckchair for nothing. I set one up and went to eat at their beach bar. Horse was on the menu. I plumped for the spaghetti alle vongole.

◆•▶

Later that afternoon we found the parts concession Luca had located. A dark warehouse on the edge of town on the airport road. Walking in from the bright sunshine, it took me a while to make out the presence of a spry man in bottle-bottomed glasses behind the counter. He told me that the part was not genuine Fiat but an aftermarket part – and at €19, a lot less than Fiat's for €120. He said he'd give me a further discount for being British.

'You'll find a lot of Italians love the English,' he said. 'We remember what you did for us during the war.'

I had experienced this warmth before, and I thanked him. It's not something you hear in France.

'You going to fit that yourself?' He asked.

I said that I had only brought a limited set of tools. Did he know somewhere?

'Let's see' he said, jumping into the passenger seat and putting his back against the waterbottles. I apologised and said I could move them, but he said not to worry, 'I am thin enough'. We drove around the corner where there were three mechanic's workshops. All very under the arches. One of them – the most world-weary of the lot – accepted the task and said tomorrow morning at nine.

'Va bene?'

◆•▶

That afternoon I wandered around the marina. Some very lovely boats. One, a beautiful sloop from Rhode Island. I sat in the shade and closed my eyes, only to be disturbed by a couple of young people who stopped in front of me to have a blazing row. It was highly acrimonious and accusatory, mostly about the boyfriend's snobby parents. She was the wounded party, but he was the one with eyes full of tears. Then very loud blasts on a horn rocked the town, echoing off the seafront hotels. A huge cruise ship, the Costa Firenze (what a dumb name), moved out from her berth.

How many souls aboard I couldn't imagine. Thousands? What a terrible way to travel. I couldn't understand it.

That night I went to a little bar and had a Campari Spritz. The waiter chatted away in perfect English. He had worked for 18 months at The Ivy, Chelsea. Not for the first time did I regret our country's decision to leave the EU.

33
THE HILL

That morning I met the distractingly pretty parking attendant who had taken to calling me 'Meester English'.

The first night's parking had been eye-wateringly expensive. But I was straight off a ferry at 10pm and tired. I had paid less for a room on several occasions. But we had got chatting over the three days and she cut me a deal. It was now a third of the price.

'Ahah' I thought. 'Beware of charm.'

I stopped off at 'Lavasecco Pony' with my washing. With a name like that it was likely to get the marks out. I think the lady asked if I wanted my underpants ironed, but I couldn't be sure.

◆

A little later, we arrived back at the garage. Cars in various states of general collapse were parked all over the shop. The tools most in use seemed to be an angle grinder and a club hammer. I delivered Pedro into their tender care.

OPERATION PEDRO

'Be brave,' I said to him. 'There won't be any anaesthetic.'

As the mechanic was draining the coolant, I asked him to put anti-freeze back in, as we were going back to Blighty. I had to use Google Translate for that one.

I sat on the bumper of a small tanker to wait in the shade, but there was a nasty smell. I realised that it was a septic tank emptying truck and got up rather quickly!

I asked the mechanic to test the fan. Despite the heat, I had never heard it come on. He revved the engine at mid-range for what seemed ages. After five minutes it cut in and we both cheered. Ridiculous really, but he was already a Pedro fan. Then I asked him to remove the rear wheel trims. The car looked odd with just two. Cleverly they were only held on by one of the four wheel bolts, so you didn't need to jack it. Something I'd never realised and had I known, I would have removed them myself. He was going to put them in the boot, but I told him they were a present for him. He muttered something and went inside. I asked the man standing next to me what he had said.

'Now all I need is a Panda missing two wheel trims,' he laughed.

I told Pedro he looked more rugged with his bare rims. We'd give the Corsa kids a run for their money once we got home.

'Oi, oi saveloy!' said Pedders.

In time all was finished and I was so grateful that I over-tipped him. As we were about to drive off he came running out of his office and stood in front of the car to stop me. OMG, I thought. What vital part has he not tightened up? But he only wanted to give me a T-shirt with the name of his garage on it. Sweet. He threw it through the open passenger window onto the passenger seat and I noticed there was a black and greasy thumb print where he had held it.

◆•▶

I walked up and out of town to the Botanic Gardens. Love a botanic garden, me.

I had sprayed up with mozzie deterrent in preparation but still 'i bastardi' got me. I hate those guys, but they love me big time. The gardens were okay as far as these – universally underfunded – institutions go. I liked the succulents best. They had planted drifts of cacti together and they had made elegant architectural formations.

SUCCULENTS IN THE BOTANICAL GARDENS, CAGLIARI

THE HILL

Coming back down there was a raised cistern filled with tall reeds which turned out to be papyrus. A couple of American ladies nearby told me that they were historians in residence at the local university and had actually created paper from last year's crop.

Then I went even further on my mission to reach maximum altitude. Passing the second-century Roman amphitheatre (closed for renovation thankfully), it was built into the hill and was extremely steep. Then a lovely Capuchin convent. And after half an hour of steady climbing in the sun, finally reaching the Museum of Modern Art.

Some Futurist paintings downstairs but up above a brilliant collection of Mino Maccari. His paintings were colourful and humorous depictions of ladies in states of undress with other characters, clowns and men in fancy dress. Very playful stuff.

Outside. A delightful public garden that put the Orto Botanico to shame. It was formal and elegant with avenues of beautiful trees and naturalistic planting that showed real creativity. Not one of those municipal jobs with beds full of garish stock plants and rows of cannas. There were more incredible views from its low walls. I sat for half an hour on a shady bench.

Down the hill and I came to a strange building. It looked like an old-fashioned telephone exchange. But people were coming out with bags. I went in and discovered an impressive market on two floors and in full swing. I found out later that this was the famous San Benedetto food market. (No? Nor me.) It is the largest indoor market in Italy.

The fish were 'stiff fresh' as Rick Stein would say.

STIFF FRESH AT THE FOOD MARKET, CAGLIARI

Everything you could want was here. Among the more eye-catching sights was a whole horse's leg and thigh hanging from a hook. Beds of cool herbs that you could spend a scented night in. And a three-metre-long swordfish, enough for the five thousand. The traders were cheerful and not shouty. It was, overall, a soothing experience. Oh, to do your daily shop here instead of a faceless but overly branded place where words like 'Finest' or 'Taste the Difference' were trademarked and tagged onto bottles, jars and cans.

34

ISLAND CROSSING

I read the news today. Oh boy! The Conservative Party was going from crisis to crisis. In Truss I did not trust. And Shapps as Home Secretary? Well, that was beyond a joke. It seemed the government couldn't run a tap, let alone the country. What an embarrassment. I switched to WhatsApp instead where some of the commentary was fruity to say the least. Meanwhile, here in Italy, and on the TV, Berlusconi and the far right's Salvini were having a cock measuring contest. Oh dearie me!

My hotel was on the front. Beyond the gardens and their giant ficus trees (we call them rubber plants at home) the town is separated from the water by roads. Two lanes of cars each way. And in the middle, bus lanes and trolley buses too. This means crossing eight lanes.

To do so, you put your faith in the zebra crossings which are generally respected. But the distractions of Facebook mean that there are sometimes a few near misses. Texting at the wheel is de rigeur. Or whatever that is in Italian. Normale?

Anyway, I hadn't had a problem until this morning when I was very nearly run down by the local Carabinieri going the wrong way up a bus lane. Their bumper literally on my shins. I definitely wasn't looking the wrong way. They waved me angrily out of the road and sped off, tyres screeching on the polished stones.

At the car park I had a look under the bonnet. The water was below minimum. Entering the bar across the street I asked to buy the bottle of water that was on the counter.

'Don't you want a fresh one?' the barman asked. I told him it was for the car and he let me have it for nothing. Pedro was now topped up with San Pellegrino. I'd parked between the two rival trucks that sold indoor plants on the parking lot. They were permanent residents, and both had a flat tyre or two.

The parking girl came over smiling and wagged her finger at me.

'Are you trying to hide from me, Mr English?!'

'Never, honey!'

It was a misty morning and she shivered despite her hoodie and quilted jacket.

'Last day I see you?' She said.

'Yep, Cala Gonone today,' I said, wiping away an imaginary tear. 'Ciao Bella.'

◄•►

Out of town the country quickly appeared. Cagliari – the Sardinian capital – really was a small town. Farmyard smells now. Manure and wild thyme and woodsmoke.

Through mountains and across the spine of the island. A Porsche came up quickly behind me. I couldn't imagine driving a car like that on these roads. Hard suspension, no clearance, low profiles. Then around the corner there was another one, stopped with white smoke pouring out of its open tail. That either meant an oil leak or a new pope. Behind him a Ferrari had stopped to lend a hand, but I couldn't imagine what they could do except phone for a breakdown truck. They were both dressed like Venetian taxi drivers on their day off. Some kind of rally, I assumed.

Pedro was silent on the matter. His brakes were whistling again. When they weren't being used. Stamping hard on the middle pedal stopped the noise for a while.

A long drive to get to the one-horse town of Cala Gonone. And the horse had bolted. I drove up to an agriturismo for lunch. Passing sheep and goats and pigs in the act of making more little pigs. Shameless. But I felt hopeful for a meaty lunch extravaganza. Unfortunately, the place was only open for dinner.

I found a decent establishment in town. Open air and looking over the beach. Red snapper and some sauteed spuds with onions. Delicious with a couple of glasses of beer.

There wasn't enough here to keep us, so we carried onwards and upwards to Alghero. Up through the mountains. With roadside warnings for snow chains. Hard to contemplate in this heat. And then across a rolling plain of scrubby bushes, tightly packed, rounded and a continuous dark green. I felt like an ant on a head of broccoli.

ISLAND CROSSING

PRICKLY PEAR, EVERYWHERE

Next came empty and dusty towns. Full of apartment blocks but not a soul about in the mid-afternoon. A single old man on a bench. A young mother pushing a pram. It was like the bomb had dropped. These places depressed me even though I was only driving through. There was not a café or a shop that I could see. It seemed a sad place to live.

Back on the plain, we went for miles on an elevated road over marshes of rushes as far as the eye could see. In the afternoon we reached Alghero and parked up for the night at the marina just outside the walls.

That evening on the lungomare, a quaint little bar. I took a Campari spritz to watch the sun go below ground, or rather the sea. On paying, the rather batty lady owner looked at me with a wistful sigh. I asked if she was a little tired?

'Quasi terminato,' she said. Almost finished. Obviously dreaming of the quieter winter months. I felt a close bond with her and smiling, rubbed her back.

35

THE TRUMAN SHOW

In the morning I bought a bottle of wine, some bread and cheese and a bar of chocolate to stock up. The lady on the checkout gave me a knowing half-smile. I wasn't sure what she meant by it but it was friendly. Perhaps she wanted to take me home and feed me some proper food?

I went to a garage to get my brakes looked at, but they couldn't fit me in until Monday morning, This was Friday. So that decided me to stay in Alghero.

A delightful place to be marooned. At times I was all alone on the sea walls, despite it being the weekend. It was as if it had been created just for me. I wondered if I ran down an alley, an alarm would wake a dozing computer designer to render a street in front of me.

By day I walked the bastioni, the giant walls left over from the Catalan control of the city. By evening there was a small buzz and I would stroll the battlements and sit overlooking the sea at one of the hole-in-the-wall bars that the locals frequent with their dogs. Both the dogs and their owners wrapped up for the weather. It was still in the mid-twenties but the wind was picking

ALL ALONE IN ALGHERO

up and there were white horses on the harbour approaches. The cardinal buoy, which must have been six feet high, was sometimes hidden by the waves, and we were at least 50 feet up.

In the distance the promontory of Fertilia, in the shape of a man lying on his back, and at the far end a lighthouse flashing its signature. A single light every four seconds.

◆•▶

The next morning there was quite a lot of damage from the wind in the night. I'd slept with all the windows open. The pendant lamp swinging shadows across the room from the street lighting outside. Waiters were retrieving tables and chairs and quite a few ambulances were rushing around making that quaint oh-lah-di-dah, oh-lah-di-dah sound.

Keeping an eye out for dog muck, I found some cash on the ground. I stuffed it in my pocket. When I counted it later it turned out to be €260. I handed it to a passing policeman. I visited a couple of churches and by this time it was getting on for lunch. Then a lot of horn honking and a parade of scooters went past. It was a wedding procession, the bride sitting side-saddle on the back of the lead Vespa, laughing. I found a man guarding the bikes later outside the cathedral.

Meanwhile in Rome, Giorgia Meloni had just been sworn in as prime minister at the Quirinale. Her far-right party – Italy's first since WWII – had formed a coalition with Salvoni's anti-immigration lot and

Berlusconi's bunch, after an election with one of the lowest voter turnouts ever.

◆•▶

That night I tucked into Zuppa di Cozze. There are mussels in abundance here and I'd been eating them off and on since Greece. Then I followed up with Porchetta. I'd passed this restaurant several times and almost got to know the owner Franco. I'd tried for a table at lunch, but they were just closing.

'Stasera?' I asked.

'Dicianove,' he replied.

So I turned up at 7pm and was looking around. The waiter deferential.

Franco emerged from nowhere and berated the waiter. The gist of it was, 'This bloke's been past four times. Get him seated right now!'

It was real old-school Italian. Like a place I used to frequent in Amersham. But the food, much better. I'd tried hard to not eat on these past days and was feeling better for it. But the days were long. This would keep me going for a week or so. I made a note to try the mussels like this at home with a mildly spiced tomato sauce. They'd be in season when I got back. But they seemed to be in season here in the Med all summer long.

On leaving, I heard Franco talking to a young chap sitting on the harbour wall, who looked like a chef, and learned that the mussels were from Spain. So, perhaps flown out from Scotland yesterday?

◆•▶

THE TRUMAN SHOW

THERESA - BAR OWNER, ALGHERO

Next day Pedders and I took a trip through the hills to Bosa, down the coast. The weather beautiful and cool on the tops. We took the Strada Mala inland, ignoring all the warning signs. It wasn't a bad road by Sardinian standards, and I'd seen worse in downtown Palermo. The country round here was all bosky, low-growing oak and sheer limestone outcrops. Over Monte Minerva with its vertiginous cliffs and lake at the bottom and on to Montresta. Everything really quiet on Sunday morning. Then down into Bosa on the coast.

CURIOUS GOATS ON THE ROAD

I sat with some locals in a bar in the shade and had a beer or two.

Afterwards, a spectacular coastal drive home. Fabulous views of the cliffs being slowly eroded by the waves like they were licking an ice cream. All along the roadside buttercups and daisies on verdant verges, the bright greens tempered by the grey sage of the mimosa.

Everything was coming into blossom, including some of the trees. It was like a second spring with the cooling of the summer. I got out to stretch my legs and a mass of butterflies on the ground made me careful as to where to place my feet. Swallowtails and Brimstones. Very pretty and warming their wings. Just hatched, I imagined.

The road was beautiful. Well, the views were. The road itself was full of holes. Someone had helpfully pointed them out with yellow spray paint, but that didn't make them any less lethal. Plus, cyclists to avoid and Sunday bikers coming up fast on their cafe racers. I just kept up a steady pace and turned the rear-view mirror to one side.

A final night. A valedictory Campari spritz from the bar owner I'd nicknamed Santa Theresa, and an early bed. Perfect.

36

AN IDEA OF ITALY

Monday morning. I was outside Andrea's garage bright and early at 0830.

'Sono qui,' I said with a grin.

'So I see,' his eyes read.

He took Pedders for a spin. Up the street I heard the ABS – and tyre adhesion – being tested to the maximum. Then he almost knocked me down as he drove into the garage at high speed – where I was waiting – and straight onto the car hoist.

Up went Pedders. Wheels hanging floppy and showing his underthings. Andrea pointed to the remains of blobby plastic on the wheel nuts. I explained about the trims melting off. I then remembered that I'd replaced the trims to tart the car up a bit with some that I had found on Ebay. I think they must have been made from recycled washing-up bowls rather than the proper heat-resistant ABS plastic. Andrea looked at me stone-faced. I said that I'd been driving on mountain roads.

'Hmmm, piano, piano,' he said.

Pedro cocked an eyebrow at me in a Gromit-like

manner. But in response I was unapologetic. He had loved tearing down those colli and screaming the tyres round the hairpins. And he knew it!

Some of you may think I've been a little wet in worrying about Pedro. But I started my life with crap cars and had mended them at the roadside. I once removed a damaged tie rod on a 2CV and bent it straight in the crook of a tree. All while wearing black tie and my date sitting in the jacked-up car out of the rain. But those days were over. Pedro, as analogue as he

PEDRO GETS HIGH

was, was now beyond me mechanically. I had a loathing for being stranded somewhere. And I wanted to keep being adventurous in the roads we took. Where both passing help and mobile signal was patchy. That called for preventative maintenance.

Andrea woke me from my daydreaming.

'There's nothing wrong,' his eyes said.

I could see there was plenty of pad left for myself. He spun the wheels to show that they weren't binding. Alrighty then. Good to go.

'Cosa ti devo?' How much do I owe you, I asked him.

'Niente,' he said.

In England I would have given him a 'drink'. But I was unsure of the etiquette of that here. So, I shook his hand and left.

◂•▸

A pleasant drive through country that reminded me of Cumbria on a sunny morning. Difficult farming. A few cows, some scattered sheep, rather welcoming in this weather. The towns we passed through, though, were all concrete and soulless.

We arrived in Santa Theresa di Gallura, pretty in a naive sort of way. I wandered around and put on some George Harrison.

'Wah wah,' he warbled in my ear.

The place was very quiet. I saw a signpost for a cinema and was intrigued enough to go and find it on the edge of town. But it had been shut since covid. There was a viewing point with a Martello tower and Corsica a blue smudge on the horizon.

In the main square I sat down to lunch. Some very harassed Germans on a day trip arrived. They ordered but service was not as they liked. Several tables of them. All making annoying scenes. Some of them had a bus to catch. Others were dismayed by not being served their order within 20 minutes of ordering. Mildly amusing schadenfreude.

Eventually they left and all was peaceful. Then an English couple almost had an argument with the waiter about whether they should order from him or inside the restaurant. He didn't understand their request and neither did I. They took off in a huff, believing they were being laughed at. Extraordinary.

Finally, a very cool, young French couple with two beautiful kids sat next to me and shared a bowl of pasta. That's the way to do it. We chattered away and had a glass of wine together. I agreed with them that there was no agenda or timeframe when you are in the company of two under four. At least if you wanted to have a relaxing time. They took it in turns to have a crafty cigarette up the street.

Later I went to find some ice cream. And got chatting to some young guys in the queue and we went for a few drinks at a back street place they knew. Where else but Italy could you find a friendly invitation like that over an ice cream?

Walking back in the gloaming it occurred to me that this was my last day in Italy. But Sardinia didn't really feel like Italy per se. I spent some time trying to think what the real Italy was, but just confused myself.

The Lovin' Spoonful sang, 'I didn't want to do it, I didn't want to break your heart'. It suited my mood.

37

CORSE TREATMENT

Another day, another ferry. This would be our ninth of the trip. Bonifacio – at the southern end of Corsica – our next stop. Just a short hop. The white cliffs of the port were towering and sheer, making the approach spectacular as we entered the natural grotto that formed the entrance. The old town citadel teetering on the edge. I spotted a crazy staircase that went all the way down the cliff face for hundreds of feet.

Pedro had been checked by customs on the Sardinian side. But now, as we disembarked, we were hauled over again, this time for what was to become an hour and a half of standing in the sun torture. It must have been training day for the customs in Bonifacio harbour.

Everything out of the car. Everything. Then a dog was sent to sniff around. Then question after question. Exact port names and arrival and departure dates for the entire trip. Most of which I had to make up, having lost track of time a while back. They wouldn't let me approach the car where my phone was.

Then they started to take the car to bits. Vents

detached. Interior light removed. Headlining pulled down and carpets up. Under the bonnet the air filter came out.

By the time it was over I had lockjaw from maintaining a friendly grin. Not my natural resting face! All the time staring at the words 'Bienvenue a Bonifacio' writ large on the dock wall.

Pedro was pissed off. I was pissed off. We whined in low gear up the very steep hill to haute ville. We were utilising all 60hp and being snappy with the gear changes. How this place had worked before steam I had no idea. Mules, I supposed.

We parked in the hotel carpark. A true luxury for once. But actually, the real luxury in places like Greece and Turkey had been to just leave the car at the roadside. These days it was always slightly stressful entering a new town with traffic limitations and parking meters that not even the locals could understand. I left Peds to his thoughts, got into my room and hit the shower.

I thought about the customs check I'd just been through. It's a weird thing when you experience situations like that. You naturally feel guilty and start to wonder if someone, somewhere, somehow, may have put something in the car without you knowing.

They'd asked if I smoked and I was delighted to tell them that I did not. Was there any alcohol in the car? 'So what if there was?!' I thought. We are in France. But I shook my head gravely. It was all very structured. Told to stand in a certain spot. Corralled by three bovver-booted customs peeps. I was tempted to make a run for it, or dive off the dock, just to see what would happen.

The only one who spoke English was the girl Fed from Porto Vecchio down the coast. She pointed to my rucksack.

'Not many clothes for two months,' she said.

'Rub-a-dub-dub,' I replied blankly.

Then she asked what day I would be leaving France.

'4th of November,' I said.

'Just in time for your birthday,' she smiled, handing me back my passport.

'Hmmmm!' I thought, inwardly annoyed.

I didn't allow myself to get cross but I felt that I'd been operated on by an unqualified medic. There are other ways of going about security without such behaviour. An experienced border force can tell whether someone's dodgy just by their body language. It's always the non-offender who pays the price.

BONIFACIO ON THE SOUTHERN TIP OF CORSICA

CORSE TREATMENT

◆•▶

The town of Bonifacio was hard to get a handle on without pitons, crampons and climbing ropes. There were views aplenty though. And the sea, miles below, so beautiful in the lovely afternoon light. The town was stacked with tourists who were being systematically taken to the cleaners. But amazingly I found a 20-euro menu that got me paté, John Dory with rice and a strawberry parfait with a glass of wine.

Having left Alghero and its obsession with fridge magnets, here the craze was for knives. Every other shop was selling knives of all shapes, sizes and lengths. And quite a few were selling only knives. Some of which were over 12 inches long. That wouldn't cut it at home.

If I had turned into a street selling only shotguns it wouldn't have surprised me. I'd carried a penknife the entire trip but had barely used it. I had read somewhere that every Corsican male carried a knife, harking back to a long history of piracy and banditry. But why you would want to pack a non-folding dagger around town I couldn't fathom.

I found a little bar with a terrific view and ordered a Campari spritz. I'd got to like this low-alcohol but punchy drink in Venice years ago. But the waitress brought me an awful version made with Aperol. The colour of a sodium streetlight.

'This is Aperol, not Campari. Sorry but I ordered a Campari spritz?'

'Yes, that's right. We only serve Aperol.' And then held her hand out for €12.

Not even a Gallic shrug to wash it down with. Tant pis.

38

BASTIA RETREAT

It hadn't rained overnight but the streets were very wet. Sea fog I guessed. There was a delicious smell of ozone and seaweed.

I retrieved Peds out of the menage and headed north. We were going all the way to Bastia and the northernmost tip of the island.

The journey was uneventful apart from a delivery driver who tailgated me for miles until I slowed almost to a stop. He then overtook in a comically massive sooty cloud of exhaust that left us blind. It was like one of those Battle of Britain gun-camera films of a Heinkel being shot down.

The road, when we were alongside the sea, was all pretty and sandy coves with attendant beach bars. Now all closed up for the season. Nice for the residents I guessed, if there were any left. The weather clear blue and 26°.

I could see why people opted for Porto Vecchio and around. We'd been to Corsica when the boys were little, but on the other coast. The windward side where the rollers came in. The beaches there were wilder. Here on the side that faced Italy it was much quieter and the sands flat and shallow.

In Bastia I found some free parking. Winner. Then I found the flat I had rented from AirBnb but it was 12 flights up. I must have missed that in the description. The views were good and looked out over the small harbour. A brightly painted yellow Corsican Ferries boat was in. On its smoke stack a bandana-wearing bandit's head, which is the motif you see repeated everywhere on the island.

The owner texted to ask if everything was okay, was I missing anything?

THE OLD PORT IN BASTIA

'Just the oxygen tent,' I replied, still puffing from the stairs.

I sat on the sofa to get my breath back and turned on the TV. Inspecteur Barnaby (Midsomer Murders) was on and there was the church in Long Crendon where I'd got married. John Nettles going into The Eight Bells next to it, where I'd had my last pint as a single man. Curious coincidence. But in my ear, a much more effective fictional Inspector said. 'Coincidence, Lewis? Really? Coincidences are the norm, Lewis.'

So true. Your fate is yours to make. But coincidence was all confused now by the spooky modern world of machine learning and the targeting of advertising. Soon AI would be guessing your mood and serving up what it thought you needed without ever having asked for it.

<・>

Bastia. The town turned out to be a gem of a place. Very liveable. Great restaurants. Shops full of high-quality stuff to eat and wear. Nice, I thought, and none of the tourist focus that I'd just experienced down south.

Past the old port was the harbour, which had traded in its fishing fleet for the plastic boats of the rich. Lining the edges were restaurants giving a feeling of the south of France of days long gone.

Beyond the harbour wall they were putting in new sea defences. Huge concrete blocks in the shape of giant asterisks were being unloaded. A diver in the water guiding them in. They would lower in one of the concrete blocks from a barge and the diver would flop over like an otter to see if it was correctly placed. He had a full-faced helmet and talked to the barge's crane operator to make adjustments, sometimes staying in position to do so. I sure hoped everyone knew what they were doing.

I found a modern and tidy restaurant in a square of plane trees and had a terrific bavette steak. The guys were very professional, and the cheese that followed, excellent. Food was improving all the time as I went north.

39

FRENCH CONNECTION

The final ferry. The tenth of the trip. I'd roughly added up the total time and it came to 78 hours of sea travel in all. This one, the Mega Express Two (inspiration clearly lacking on her naming day!) from Bastia to Nice, where I hoped the welcome would be a little warmer and they wouldn't mistake my little donkey for a mule.

At the port, a few hundred rental cars were waiting dockside to be returned to the mainland. I got speaking to a guy in the lane next to me. He had 500,000 kilometres on his VW van's clock. He asked where I'd been. I said I was coming back overland from Turkey.

'You went all that way in a Fiat?'

'How rude!' Pedro and I jointly thought.

I said I'd race him to be onboard first. We were both lined up at the front of the grid. He revved his engine. The gates opened but the woman waved me on first.

'Haha,' I shouted out of the window. 'Eat my dust..!'

‹•›

FRENCH CONNECTION

PILOT DROP OFF IN NICE ROADS

Onboard, the usual palaver, but finally found a steward and got installed. A very nice cabin which was not really necessary. But it came with the ticket.

The bar area was already full. I ordered a coffee. Almost every table had a card game going on. Maybe this was the Bastia Hold'em or Fold'em Society's day cruise?

The entire crew was Italian. I wasn't sure why that was either, on a vessel owned by Corsican Ferries.

◆•▶

We rounded Cap Ferrat and there was Nice. Quite low-rise in comparison to Monaco, which we had just passed. A brown smudge of pollution held in by the hills behind. But the town, good-looking in the early evening sunlight. The pilot boat scudded out to meet us across the millpond sea.

That night, moules mariniere and a racy white to accompany. Then a post-prandial amble along the prom. This is where that madman had taken out all those poor people by running them down with his truck. I had plenty to dodge here, what with rollerblades and guys doing tricks on bikes. Lots of people about on this balmy evening and circles of young people on the beach with lanterns and guitars.

The prom itself though, lit by LED streetlamps. There is something strange about that lighting that makes everything seem very flat and grainy.

◆•▶

FRENCH CONNECTION

Oh, what a night! And I don't mean in a Frankie Valli way. The hotel room was one of the smallest – and one of the most expensive – of the trip, but I figured this was just a pit stop.

However, it was a very hot night. The air conditioning wasn't working so I opened the windows and the racket from below was intolerable. I shut them again.

Then at 2am the club across the street really ramped up. The bass was moving the curtains. I put my ear plugs in but you could still feel the vibration. I looked out of the window. It was called KWARTZ Club. Another brilliant name.

A couple were canoodling in a doorway. Then a fight broke out. All a bit handbags at dawn, the combatants clearly drunk and swinging for victory.

Out of the club came a man who looked like he was made from boulders. One of the original Fantastic Four, perhaps? The girlfriend of the kissing couple now behind her man and the two of them watching.

Boulder boy had what I thought was a fire extinguisher. But it turned out to be pepper spray. He doused the local boxing club, who ran off, rubbing their eyes, to a street corner.

I dozed. Then les flics arrived mob-handed. Eight of them in two vans. Blue lights filling my room. I gave up on sleep. By this time, it was four o'clock. I caught up on four episodes of a slow-burn Korean police drama I had been watching on Netflix.

In the morning I was asked about my evening. I told the concierge all about it and he deducted my parking and gave me a discount. He apologised about the air conditioning. From what I gathered there was a city-wide ban on AC use after mid-October.

'Not just this hotel sir… all hotels in France.'

◆•▶

On the road, we travelled the length of Nice's bay boulevard. Several kilometres then we turned right over a clover leaf to the A8 for 280 kilometres. Just the one road all the way to Orange.

We passed all those famous names like Cagnes and Antibes and Cannes and then Marseille, where we turned north.

The hues of the countryside here, and the earth embankments where the road cut through, was all yellows and whites, ochres and oranges. These were the colours of the French Impressionists. Their landscapes, that always look a little out there and garish colour-wise, were actually quite accurate.

'I paint what I see,' Manet had said.

◆•▶

Orange. I'd last been here with Teddy after the successful location of his egg-packer girlfriend from Bradford. Then it had been a dusty little place with not much going on. I'd thought it charming and was pleased to find it still so now.

We'd put his Cortina up on a kerb and stayed at Le Glacier Hotel overlooking the market square, where we proceeded to spend the night with some local lads drinking Kanterbrau.

It had been a cranky little hotel. And the whip-thin

lady owner took a liking to us and made a special effort. She'd given me a great room overlooking the square and I'd felt like a prince. Especially after some of the accommodation we'd experienced on that trip.

The hotel was still there but not as charming now that they'd thrown out the pale blue shutters and installed plate glass.

Also still there was the incredibly well-preserved 1st-century Roman theatre. When Teddy and I had visited it had been practically derelict. We'd sort of broken our way in through corrugated iron on an adjoining building and wandered around. Downright dangerous in parts. I wondered if he still had any of his Super 8 film of us clowning around inside?

ROMAN AMPHITHEATRE, ORANGE

Now it was used for opera festivals and had been fully restored. I could have paid to go in but didn't. The Glacier was full, so I went to 'Le Grand', a Best Western on a back street.

They gave me an appalling room with a view of the air conditioning units covered in bird dirt. And the air conditioning didn't work either! When I enquired at reception they moved me to their best room. So kudos for that.

Later that evening I took a stroll through the honey-coloured streets. Still glowing after the autumn sunshine. Lots of kids were in costume celebrating Halloween, although they were two days early.

As I passed the Glacier they were having a lively salsa evening. Everyone out and dancing on the street.

40

HOT STUFF

Before I left Orange, and not knowing when I'd be back, Pedders and I went for a hack around the town.

I'd had a fantastic night of sleep. Cold outside and all my windows open. Duvet up to the chin. Just my coconut skull showing.

It was a stunning morning with just a wisp of mist. Peds started up okay but there was that judder from the clutch. He'd be fine once he'd got the blood pumping.

Away from the main drag it was really lovely and obviously wealthy. Planted – and carefully looked after – verges and avenues of pollarded trees. Elegant boxy villas, all very beautiful in the perfect morning.

We found the triumphal arch on the outskirts. First-century Roman and built during the time of Augustus. Intricately carved friezes in deep relief adorn it and the arch is in great condition considering its age. Once this place had been on the Agrippan Way. What must it have been like then? So fascinating to think about those times. What, for that matter, would Londinium have been like? On that mound where the City of London

ROMAN TRIUMPHAL ARCH, ORANGE

sits today. However you approach the City, you always have to walk uphill.

◆•▶

A longish drive of 476 kilometres. But on these roads, not a problem. Right at the end I had a mishap with the final toll. It wouldn't accept my ticket. I pressed the button for help, which alerted all the other drivers in the queues alongside to gape at this idiot Rosbif. But it also caused a very charming blonde lady to dismount from her Range Rover, nimbly hop over the barrier and berate the man on the intercom.

He was saying something about moving my car forward. I looked at the blonde. We both knew this was BS. Then he said something about a blue light. This light always flashed to show where to put your ticket. She told him 'no blue light showing.'

Meanwhile I was at the back of the car, chopping fingers across my neck to stop other cars entering my lane. They would see me at the last moment and comically swerve to another lane. All very Jacques Tati.

Now the cars in her lane were honking their horns because she was holding them up, too. But she was too cool to worry.

Finally, the operator must have reset the booth because the blue light came on. Madame wished me well, blew me a kiss on both cheeks and hopped it to her motor before I could even thank her. The barrier was up. I hadn't paid. The man was shouting on the intercom but I wasn't listening. Pedders flew out of the gate like a greyhound after the rabbit. I couldn't stop him… honest!

We'd passed Lyon to the south. A stunning road crossing the Rhone, twice. I'd been on this route before but couldn't remember all this and must have bypassed it somehow. The road north was four lanes of bumper-to-bumper traffic flowing smoothly in and around and over the river. It was heavily regulated by speed controls, which seemed to be working well at rush hour. It looked like such a vibrant and industrialised city that I knew I would return. This is what I like, a town with purpose, not just some stuck-in-aspic tourist trap. But then I thought, Venice is surely exactly that, and you're a massive fan. I reminded myself that nowadays I only went for the Biennale, which gave that city a purpose, too.

Pedders was getting thirsty (as was I) as we passed signs for Beaune and Gevry Chambertin and Nuits St George. Then a sign saying welcome to Dijon… 'cite de gastronomia et vin.' I didn't need any more urging.

◆•▶

Dijon, a truly dull town on the outskirts, was mostly closed on a Sunday. Local ordinance perhaps?

In the hotel it was as hot as the hobs of hell. I asked at reception. They said all AC was now off until next summer.

'But would you like us to turn the heating down?'
'Would I?!'

◆•▶

The historic centre is a beautifully preserved mix of timber-framed medieval town houses, sitting cheek by jowl with gothic churches and renaissance masterpieces. The main square is a spectacular and wide expanse of stone. It holds the Ducal Palace (this being the home of the Dukes of Burgundy) and opposite that a semi-circle of arches, now glassed-in and turned into restaurants.

It was here that I found a brilliant meal. They were turning the tables fast. The waitress came to take my food order but, when I ordered a Ricard and waved her away, I saw her interrogated by the head of service. She then decided I was not to be rushed and I proceeded to have a very fine and relaxed meal. Ouefs a la muerette (poached eggs in a white wine and epoisses cheese

MAQUETTE FOR RUDE'S ARC DE TRIOMPHE SCULPTURE

sauce) followed by a confit duck and lentil salad. The meal lasted two hours, for me at least. In which time I saw the covers change almost completely. At the end I tried to tip her but her professional pride wouldn't allow it.

◆•▶

Now it was time for a stroll.

Twenty or so dog owners of the town were having a little Sunday training outing, and put on a show for the al fresco diners. All of them – and some of their dogs – in very fancy and theatrical costumes.

I popped into the 'Rude Museum'. It had plaster casts of some giant sculptures. The showcased sculpture adorning the rear wall of this former church was impressively rude. Giant revolutionary characters surrounding a naked man with his penis at head height. A gaggle of girls were taking it in turn to be photographed beside it. It looked vaguely familiar and I read that this was just a plaster maquette. The actual sculpture was to be found on the side of the Arc de Triomphe in Paris. Apparently Monsieur Rude – the sculptor – was a Dijon home boy. His work can be seen on monuments all around Paris.

Then I went into Notre Dame, the cathedral, and lit yet another candle for the deceased cat. It was a typically big old gothic job but had some flooring to die for. I spent a pleasant afternoon wandering around the public buildings and visiting small galleries, until my room cooled down and I could rest without sleeping in the shower. There were a lot of families about, enjoying the sunny weather. But without the shops open it felt a little strange to me. We relaxed those laws, especially in major towns, so long ago that I wasn't sure about it.

41

BACK IN THE 8TH

Another beautiful day, but now too cold to have the windows down. I had been so lucky with the weather. How long could it last? Oops, I thought to myself, now I've gorn and seddit.

◆•▶

The breakfast was included at the hotel. They had a novel egg-boiler that let you lower your own eggs inside a cradle. I put the timer on my phone and went to make some toast. When I came back after five minutes one of my eggs was missing. Now, what kind of person.?! 'VOLEUR!'

I settled for one egg but in truth I hate these buffet affairs and tend to avoid them. Everyone being overly polite.

'After you.'

'No, after you, please.'

'No, no, no. After you. I insist!'

Gimme a break. And everyone constantly milling around. I just wished they would simply sit down and get on with it.

BACK IN THE 8TH

PADLOCKS OF LOVE ON THE PONT DES ARTS

QUINTESSENTIALLY FRENCH – RICARD WITH A LITTLE ICE AND WATER

On the road. Beautiful autumnal colours. The grosgrain fields ready for winter planting, contrasting with the turning leaves. The French road signs as usual all reading like a menu. Epoisses followed by Chablis. Throw in a baguette and you'd have the makings of a decent picnic.

Another 340 kilometres and we were into Paris and alongside the Seine. The Eiffel Tower on the right. Then across Place de la Concorde and up to La Madelaine and then down underneath her skirts to park in Rue Tronchet car park.

It was from this very carpark that my friend Nigel had retrieved my Ford Cosworth without a ticket all those years ago. He'd talked a good story and driven the car out. Good going because at the time Sapphire Cossies were the most frequently stolen car in Europe. I'd had a job getting the thing insured. I suspect he went for a little tootle around in it over the slippery cobbles. So, I was glad he hadn't lost me my no-claims bonus.

That afternoon was all glorious sunshine. I did what everyone else was doing and went for an amble. I avoided the Champs Elysees. That was an evening thing for me. Not sure why I felt that. Anyway, instead I turned left at Concorde and walked the length of the Tuileries.

By and by I came to Le Pont des Arts. I had got down on my knees here and asked my then girlfriend to marry me. G only hesitated for a beat, but it was a heart-stopping moment. While I was down there a couple of Japanese girls came and took a photo of us and ran off giggling. In those days it had scruffy chain-link on the sides. And later, couples took to putting padlocks on it until the weight became so great that the chain-link was removed and replaced with glass. But people still found secret places to put them. Love always finds a way.

Further on, Notre Dame. Still a work in progress after the great fire and would be for some while. Stacked portacabin offices were lodged high up on the roofline, looking incongruous.

I found one more fake Mona Lisa at one of those book stands that line the embankment. And later a T-shirt of Mona Lisa doing a dab. Leonardo, after all his achievements, what a terrible painting to be remembered for.

That evening it rained hard. I told you I'd jinxed it.

42

ALL SAINTS

Up with Eos and out into a magnificent day of clear sunshine. I wandered down through the deep shade of Rue Royale, past Maxim's and strode out into the blazing light of Place de la Concorde. As I rounded the corner of the Hotel de Crillon a very fresh breeze made me wonder why I had left my jacket behind. I could have nipped back but didn't want to miss any of this light, so I thought I'd risk it. The arch at the top of the Champs Elysees called me and I couldn't resist it.

There weren't many folk about yet. This was All Saint's Day, a national holiday. It had scuppered my plans for museums which I would now have to cram into tomorrow. When I got to L'Etoile I went to look at M. Rude of Dijon's sculpture on the side.

◆•▶

I took the Metro for the heck of it. I wanted to get to the Eiffel Tower but the 6 wasn't running so I did a workaround. Ridiculous really. Up to Place de Clichy and then down to Invalides where I was going to catch the RER. But someone had decided that All Saint's Day was their day to exit this earthly realm and had thrown themselves across the tracks. I walked out onto the quai where the sunshine made it hard to even contemplate suicide.

Walking over the Pont d'Alexander the Bat-O-Bus (actually a great name) was getting up steam. I hopped on and we went downstream to M. Eiffel's vertical Forth Bridge. This was proper tourist stuff, but it was fun. We got a grebe's eye view of the houseboats and wondered what that kind of life was like.

The 'bus' – with the handling attributes of a punt – performed a messy U-turn and puttered off in the other direction. I got off an hour later at Jardin des Plantes and sunk a quick Ricard before starting the walk back.

Ile St. Louis is one of those really romantic places, at least it always had been for me, and conjured up those heady days with G before the kids came along.

I stopped at La Brasserie de l'Isle – on the point facing Citè – and had a superb and fluffy omelette with a green salad. And a glass of red Sancerre to go with it. It's a Flemish-styled place on the end of Ile St Louis so its name is a play on words.

The leaves were turning outside. The wine had made me drowsy. I hailed a cab on the embankment. I wasn't sure that's how you got a taxi but he stopped anyway. Moaning how bad business was on a bank holiday.

That evening I strolled down to Pont d'Alma where the Bateau Mouches were moored and caught another scenic tour of the river. Perfect timing. The boat ready to go and the sun only just down. The Catherine

Deneuve (I would have preferred the Isabelle Adjani, but beggars can't be choosers) had 1,000 tourists on board. A great raft of a thing. The bridges were pretty, and it was still warm enough for just a sweatshirt. Hard to credit it was now November.

'A superb row of mansion houses typical of the Belle Epoque vernacular,' said the stilted voice on the PA.

'The Seine has always been a major commercial thoroughfare. Here we are 395 miles by water to the sea.'

I tapped noise cancelling on my earpods and tuned it out with some Gérard Depardieu songs. The dear old tower was lit up in the colour of a Golden Rain firework. What a day. It made me think about what I had planned for tomorrow and to abandon it. So beautiful was this lovely city that simply walking its streets was a luxury. And after all, I was an Englishman and always carried my umbrella.

43

A MUSÉE

Sitting in a café at breakfast, on the corner opposite Fauchon, I watched the office workers hurry past. Ping! It was a text from Brendon.

'Just woken up in the UK, three prime ministers later.'

He said he was having the full English with black pudding. I looked at my plate of deux oeufs plat and accompanying salad. It didn't bear comparison.

I took the 12 under the river, direction Mairie d'Issey, and got off at Solferino. A beautifully tiled station. Some Metro stations were like this and others terribly scruffy. I wondered what governed that.

This was a pleasant neighbourhood, just south of the Musee d'Orsay, and I made a note to think about this area for a stay – Rive Gauche – on another occasion.

While I waited in the queue for the gallery I contemplated whether the life-sized rhino sculpture next to me had a pet detective escaping from its rear.

Getting here at opening time proved effective and I headed straight for the Post Impressionists on the fifth floor. Passing an impressive café on the way.

CLOCK WINDOW – MUSEE D'ORSAY

I filled up on Gaugin, Degas, Monet and Van Gogh, and loved a painting by Lautrec called simply, Le Lit, of two kids sleeping in a bed.

Then I went downstairs and bagged some of my favourite artist, Camille Corot. Nobody paints trees like him. But in truth there were better ones in the Ashmolean back home.

And then by happy chance, I found there was an Edvard Munch exhibition on. It was incredible and worth a trip to Paris in itself. I didn't have a ticket for it and blagged my way in. It was, however, horribly crowded and stuffy, which was a shame. Some of his later works were stupendous and obviously autobiographical. The artist staring back at you in baggy trousers and braces. These were giant works and freely painted. I was impressed.

I lit out onto the river and looked for a bar to do a bit of research, eventually deciding on the Museum of Modern Art. There was no easy train, so I hailed a green-lit cab. He wanted to take me to the Louvre and drove back towards Concorde.

'No, no, that's the wrong way. Pont d'Alma!'

'Ah. You want the Museum of African Art,' he said.

'Certainly not. Here, look at the map on my phone, mate.'

When we got there, a huge white edifice right on the embankment, I mumbled that it was hard to miss. He laughed and said that nobody had ever asked him to take them there before.

And when I got in I realised why. A pretty second-rate permanent collection that was not worth missing the sunshine for. But I fell for a painting by Soulages. A giant canvas three metres by two – impossible to photograph – and the size of my allotment shed. He'd scumbled in some grisaille and laid on beautiful black with such confidence. A woman next to me saw me goggling at it and asked me what I thought. I told her that I wished that I could paint like this. She was a lecturer at a local university and a painter herself. She said she only came here to view this painting. And we agreed that it was the strongest work in the gallery.

Sauntering back, I dawdled through a stunning farmers' market. Imagine coming here and deciding what to cook that night from what looked good. Rather than making a list and then finding that your local Sainsbury's didn't stock half of it?

'Veal chops sir? No. Never had any call for those, sir. Have you looked in the pre-pack section?'

After a croque madame I stretched my legs down the Seine and did a bit of sunbathing – with my clothes on – in a sheltered spot.

◆•▶

My last night in Paris. It had been a mad day of angry traffic. It was still going now, at 7pm. All day there had been police and ambulances rushing everywhere. Snarling the traffic and making everyone lean on their horns. This was a city that could quickly boil over and I'd been caught up in a nasty demonstration once in the past. On the other hand, I'd brought the boys here the day after a crazy night of rioting and looting and there was no trace of it. It had been big enough to make the news headlines, but nothing to see the next day.

A MUSÉE

Keep it together guys, until I exit.

I bade a fond farewell to Le Colibri café, who had made me feel really at home. Tonight, I was going to a little bistro that had been suggested, Le Petit Vendome.

This place was the real deal. I ordered the *Blanquette* and a *pichet* of mid-price burgundy. St. Joseph in fact. Superb. Then a *tarte tatin* to die for… if it didn't kill you first. Cripes! I was going to have to take myself in hand after all this. Perhaps liposuction? I refused the waitress's siren call of cheese. But, God, it looked good. And repaired to my digs for an early night.

Adieu maitresse… jusqu'à la prochaine fois.

WAITER AT LE COLIBRI

44

LENS OF HISTORY

Lens, twenty minutes north of Arras, where I was staying for my final night of the trip. My gourmand friend Nigel had recommended Arras so I knew it would be a safe bet. I was kind of killing time because I couldn't check in to my hotel until four o'clock. These check-in times were getting silly, and later and later as I travelled north.

Lens. I'd read that there was a good gallery here – a satellite of the Louvre – but I was all arted out after yesterday, so I skipped that. I headed instead for Vimy.

◆•▶

That morning, in rush hour Paris, I had a very close call with a scooter driver. I had been checking all mirrors very carefully because the bikes were flowing through the cars at three times the speed. This guy was on my left passenger window. I indicated then moved right. In a split second he had braked and come up on my right. Gesticulating at me. I shook my fist at him, an idiot. A very close shave for him. I thought there are the quick and the dead. And then there are the dead quick. Or at least a bloody long time in hospital.

The electronic sign on the gantry read 'Peripherique Fluide'. Merci! The A1 north, very tight but still moving fast. After Charles de Gaulle the traffic thinned out to a more relaxing concentration.

◆•▶

The Canadian memorial on the 'Ridge' north of Arras is one of the most affecting monuments to the tragedy of war. It has the right balance of elegant beauty, hauteur

CANADIAN WWI MEMORIAL AT VIMY

and impenetrable sadness that makes it impossible not to be emotionally involved. Typically, big limbed – and breasted – grieving mothers – or angels – in the revolutionary style adorn it.

It was blowy and cold. Just a trace of rain in the air slapping my face sideways as I took the long way round.

'You've not brought very good weather with you!'

I hadn't heard the monument guardian behind me because of the wind and he startled me. He'd addressed me in English, which I suppose was a safe bet as this was a monument to Canadians.

'No, I left it behind in Paris. Sorry about that.'

I told him I'd had dinner on the street in shirt sleeves yesterday and he said the weather was always extreme here. The easterly blowing towards us was compressed by the slow slope of the ridge. It was similar to a tsunami effect and certainly kept the flies off.

We bantered a bit and then a young couple with two girls came up looking for their great- great-grandfather's name. The guide gave the girls Canadian flags to wave and they ran around the monument with the innocence of their youth.

I detoured back to the 14-18 Museum. This was a relatively new black box of a WWI experience centre and quite well done. There were a few, really telling, graphics. Especially one showing troop losses for French, English and American troops versus those of the Germans. Huge spikes for our offences against steady but far lower numbers for the German defenders. We were out in the open while they were dug in waiting for us. They were still digging up bones and ordnance in the fields around here, 100 years later.

There was a lovely tribute to Wilfred Owen and his poem Dulce et Decorum Est written out in full. It should be taught to every schoolboy the world over. He'd died right at the end of the war, a week before the armistice. Outside there were cemeteries everywhere. And trenches and craters, now covered with pines, furred over with grass cropped short by sheep. I looked out across the salient. Was this the only way this campaign could have been fought?

On the skyline several, gigantic pyramids. Google told me these were coal mine tailings. Basically, slag heaps that had now received UNESCO listing. What the?

After the war, the towns were devastated. It took until the end of the 1920s to get any semblance of reality back. This massive basin of coal needed men to mine it and Polish immigrants were brought in by the hundred thousand to do so. They hadn't known what to do with these giant slag heaps, so they'd turned them into monuments.

I dropped back to Arras. Cemetery after cemetery. Some with the comic bravado of names such as Cabaret Rouge.

Along the way, big combines were harvesting the sugar beet. It was piled up in pointed barrows kilometres long. The colour and resemblance of human skulls.

◆•◆

Arras. You could see the Flemish influence. Two major squares with brick mansions and bell gables all around. Not to my liking but impressive all the same.

They were tooling up for a film festival at the end of the week so I parked underground and made for my room.

That night, drunks shouting in the square below, echoing against the old merchant buildings. But then some lumpy rain made them clear off to their beds. I'd actually been woken by the banner advertising the film festival flapping in the wind outside my window. I went out onto the balcony and tied it back onto the railing. It was a wild night and I stood there for quite a while, in the building's lee, watching the festival's marquee luffing up like Cutty Sark making a tack.

After a while I couldn't feel my feet so, for the first time, I put on the cashmere socks that my daughter had given me and got back under the duvet.

45

ADIEU

A l'eau, c'est l'heure

As he boarded the longboat to be rowed ashore to St Helena, Napoleon said (in French ofc), 'To the water, it is time.' Which to an English ear sounds like, 'Allo, sailor.'

Even though I had found much to amuse me on this little journey, I had missed the English humour.

Napoleon had been born on an island and been desperate to get off it. He had finished up on another in the Atlantic's Central Channel.

I had never thought of my island home as being imprisoning. I lived close to an airport. I could be in a European city in a matter of hours. But that was before Covid. It had trapped us all and I had tried not to think about it in a claustrophobic way. Of course, getting anywhere during the Napoleonic wars had also been a major undertaking for an English tourist.

But now it did feel strange to me that I would be coming back to my small country. The sceptred isle. Shining like a jewel. Set in a silver sea. Shakespeare must have had a drone.

The dislocation of air travel was what I had been at pains to avoid. With my little donkey I had kept my feet on the ground and experienced distance and time in a realistic way. Instead of being hit by a wall of humidity at the aircraft's door, it had been a more gradual process. And also, one in a changing season, summer into autumn.

People had said, 'Why not fly out and rent a car when you get there?' But that was to miss the point. It was the getting there that was the really interesting bit for me.

And then, where exactly was 'there' anyway? I suppose you could say that it was the bit where I had stopped going east and started to return home? On a map that would probably be some unmarked sheepfold in Western Anatolia. But again, I had never really thought about it in such terms. I had used the satnav sparingly and barely even looked at a map.

Two months was the longest I had ever travelled. If anything, it had felt a very short time. For weeks, I had moved to a new place every day. But had tried to slow it down and experience some places in greater detail. That had been at the expense of the journey though and I had raced through France as if I knew it backwards. In truth, as I admitted to a friend, I didn't know France that well. I hadn't even been on these routes since before all my years of married life.

And then there were those places where I'd immediately felt at home. That I could have stayed put in for months, or even a year or so. Those temptations I had avoided too. I knew that Brendon had felt the same. To stop journeying. To 'deck down for a bit,' as he'd put it.

All of life is a compromise and every decision a selfish one. I'm not sure if that was a stoical – or even a good – philosophy, but it is one that I use all the time to explain to myself why I am here at all.

Importantly, it was the perspective it had given me. It really is a wide world out there and full of wonders. But more than that, it was the people I had met. The girl who laughed at the supermarket till. Or the friendly traveller in the ferry queue.

‹•›

LAST FRIDGE MAGNET SPOT OF THE TRIP

Now up the A26, through rain to the Channel Tunnel and back home to dear old Blighty. The land of warm beer and Chapsticks and Brussels sprouts and Wycombe Wanderers.

I had arrived way too early. They put me on a slightly earlier departure, but I still had 90 minutes before boarding.

A dreadfully boring passenger terminal building. Full of bad things to eat and buy. Fridge magnets with French flags and hearts, Je t'aime Paris, etc.

And bizarrely, a big rack of Michelin maps for France, when everyone here was going the other way, to England.

I thought balls to this. So, I got into Pedro and we made a break for the border. It was a bit iffy because they'd asked an extra 70 quid to get on this departure. But they just waved us through. It was hardly crowded.

Parked up on the train, I asked a French woman in the car in front if she knew what time we would arrive. She was just coming out of the loo and was hitching up her woolly tights through her dress, which I somehow found charming.

'It's supposed to get there at ten-twenty but in my experience it's completely random!'

I crossed my fingers at her.

'Oui monsieur, that's what I always do, too.'

Outside the tunnel, England was having a sunny day. The M26 and M25 the usual death by a thousand cut-ups.

I drove back into my town over the bridge and my daughter had put out 'Welcome home' balloons on the gate and porch. Sweet! She helped me in with my bags, which weren't many. Despite having the car, I really had travelled light. We walked up the High Street to the pub and talked over a pint. And then we went back, so I could cook my working wife a spag-boll to welcome her home on a Friday night.

I could tell that not a lot of cooking had gone on in my absence. The knives were still sharp.

The new cat had grown big. The leaves were gathering in the garden and I took my shoes off to appreciate the feel of carpet. East, West, home's best.

EPILOGUE

When I got back people asked me for impressions. But it was so hard to sum up. Some of them assumed I had gone off to find myself. To me that was simply inane. But then I felt like that about a lot of things that others found important. Like football and wristwatches.

Others were surprised that I hadn't lost weight. As if I'd been off on some sort of cure.

The most memorable parts I suppose were the little hardships, but they were also the most difficult to relate without sounding like a moaner.

The solitary side of it had meant that encounters with others became really important and I had made some good friendships. It meant that you had to work harder at things. Rather than just skim over the surface as a tourist would.

But being alone had been very freeing. What companion would have put up with stooging around on a dockside for six hours waiting for a ferry? Or driving through the night for no acceptable purpose other than the hell of it? Or going without eating for a

EPILOGUE

couple of days because it suited me? Only Pedro could put up with these behaviours – and perhaps, in his laconic way, enjoy them? He was an ascetic monk at heart. If he hadn't been built in Turin, he could have been a Japanese ronin.

DAVID, THE CAT HAD BEEN A MERE INK BLOT WHEN I LEFT

I didn't know how many miles we'd covered. Around six thousand I reckoned. One of Pedro's foibles was to reset the trip counters and clock every now and again. Whether that was random humour or a matter of privacy on his part, he wasn't saying.

It was a Saturday, November the fifth fireworks and Monday my birthday.

On Sunday, G cooked me roast beef for lunch and followed it with apple and blackberry crumble.

Now, how did she know that was my favourite?

The End

ACKNOWLEDGEMENTS

My thanks to my wife for her continued understanding and forbearance. And thanks to Ed and Rob and Christian and James for their thoughts, comments and encouragement.

Quotation from The Traveller's Guide to Classical Philosophy by John Gaskin, Thames and Hudson, 2011, reproduced with the kind permission of the author.